The Idea Friendly Guide

Practical, Immediate Steps to Break Free from Old-Way Thinking and Transform Your Community's Future

Becky McCray

SAVE
YOUR
.town

SaveYour.Town/Books

Table of contents

The Idea Friendly Creed

What we believe about small towns

We are a community of possibilities, not of problems. We are action takers. We are optimistic.

It's not about what this town used to be. We have people right now, assets right here, and we can take action right away. We don't need another plan, another committee, or another meeting. We can do it now.

We create the moments that show what this town could be and the places that take our breath away, if only just for a moment. What we create doesn't have to be permanent to create possibility.

We don't care about titles or who holds official positions. The people who do hold titles may not think like us. That's ok. No one can stop us from doing the little things that really matter.

We'd rather help 10 people try their own ideas than to hold a vote and tell everyone to support the "winner." That might be more efficient, but efficiency isn't our goal. Community is our goal. And we try everyone's ideas.

We don't let statistics and negative reports beat us up. Those numbers are nothing but a snapshot in time. What we do next is up to us.

We aren't changing our town to attract others to come save us. We are valuing the people who are here now and what we all want to create together.

That means everyone, every single one. People of all ages, all ethnicities, all backgrounds, all incomes, people who are new in town and people who have been here for generations. All of us have ways of doing things, culture and things to share. We all want a thriving town with a future for generations.

We thrive by doing more business together. We celebrate the entrepreneurs, business people, dreamers, makers, artists, experimenters, performers, crafters, bakers, upcyclers, junkers, people who sell in booths and homes and parking lots and trucks and sheds. Together we prosper, right here where we are.

We have everything we need. We are creating the community we want one small step at a time.

It's nothing short of a revolution in how we build our town together.

Welcome to an Idea Friendly town.

Why I wrote this

I'm Becky McCray, co-founder of SaveYour.Town. I wrote this book because small towns have a future. I know because I've been a small town store owner, city administrator for a town under 1,000 people, and a life-long cattle rancher. I make my home in Hopeton, Oklahoma, population 30. I don't just talk about rural issues, I live them.

Download your own copy

A printable PDF of this Creed is available at:

IdeaFriendly.com

Print it out, add your town name and hang it up. Or post to your favorite social sharing sites. The goal is to attract people who want to be Idea Friendly and spur more conversations.

There's also a video version with narration by SaveYour.Town cofounder Deb Brown and me that you can share with friends or a group. It's on that same page.

Introduction

Fear of failure traps us in the old way

In Miller, South Dakota, a high school student named Abby stood in front of a meeting room full of adults to present a new idea. She and her friends wanted an indoor movie theater. There's a drive-in theater nearby, but there's no indoor movie theater in Miller. Because the population is about 1,400 people, this is going to be a challenge.

As Abby excitedly shared this idea, one of the adults said to her, in front of everyone, "That idea is too big. It's never going to work. You shouldn't even try."

I'd like you to be shocked, but I'm sure you're not. Because people have done this to you, too, haven't they? We've all heard those brick walls that people throw in our way. "We tried that once." "That's not how we do things." "That is never going to work." "Slow down. Let us ask more questions." "Give us more time to talk it over."

When you were reading the Creed with all those positive statements of what your town could be, did you hear echoes of times when people threw brick walls in your way? Were you wishing that your town could be like that, but torn because you feel like it won't ever change?

I've felt that way about my town more times than I would like to admit.

We're going to break through those brick walls, together.

We're going to do it because you deserve a chance for a better community, just like Abby deserved the chance to try her idea.

Do you think the adult hated Abby? Were they secretly scared she would succeed? It took me awhile to realize, but now I think they wanted to protect Abby. The adult's life experience made them feel that a movie theater was unlikely to succeed as a business in Miller. They thought Abby was setting herself up to fail, and it would be embarrassing for her. In order to protect her, they told her not to even try.

And I think it's the same reason that people tell you things like "We tried that once," or "That is never going to work." They're worried that you might fail, so they're trying to help by slowing you down and pointing out the risks.

It's no wonder people say these things. We've drummed this need to avoid failure into everyone, repeatedly. We've built up the structures and methods that try to keep us from failing. School groups taught us to elect officers and think in annual calendars. Community clubs reinforced by-laws and multiple committees. Workplaces emphasized approval processes and hierarchies. Every institution delivered the same message: slow down, get permission, avoid the risk of failure.

This well-meaning advice has trapped our communities in outdated ways of working together.

People tell me how trapped they feel. "My town is hopeless." "The council won't let us do this." "This local group is useless." In our Survey of Rural Challenges, over 2,200 people from towns across the US, Canada and beyond shared the same frustrations.

Different people, different places, same exact brick walls.

You're already building community

People also tell me that what they're doing now for their community doesn't count, because they've been told it doesn't. But you do count.

You're probably already doing more to build your community than you realize.

Have you helped a neighbor? Picked up trash? Shared something positive about your town online? Supported a local business? Made a donation of time or money? Bought from a kids' fundraiser? Attended an event and cheered? Volunteered for something, even if it felt small?

That's community building. You're already part of it.

You might be comparing yourself to the community builders of a generation or two back: the ones who belonged to every club, who built the buildings, who shaped the town you see today. But comparing yourself to the past is a trap because a lot has changed.

The problem isn't that you need to start doing something bigger or more important. The problem is that the methods you've been taught trap you in outdated approaches.

I realized the methods were broken, not me

I wasn't kidding when I said I had felt frustrated at my community, too.

My turning point was when I was fired as a city administrator for trying too many new ideas. That made me angry, and I spent years after that looking for better methods for small towns. I started reading up on what successful people and communities were trying. And because I was burned out with volunteering for organizations and serving on boards, I quit all that and started experimenting with doing things informally, without the committees and planning.

Instead of "How can I get the organization to go along with this idea?" I started asking "What method would actually work today?"

While our clubs and governments and organizations are busy trying to avoid failure through endless planning and committee work, the world is changing around us. It's time for our methods to change, too.

You can let go of these old ways

You don't have to use those outdated ways of working any longer. *You can use methods designed for today.*

You don't need to struggle with difficult people. *Those are not your people.*

You don't need permission from resistant leaders. *99% of the best things you can do don't require anyone's permission.*

You don't need to fix your broken community. *It's not broken. People are using broken methods because that's how they've been taught for years.*

The possibilities in the Creed are not fantasy. *This is what happens to your community when you shift specific behaviors.*

You can transform your community by taking small steps, starting now, without waiting for permission, support or perfect conditions.

Here's the Idea Friendly Method

With all those realizations, I outlined a simple method, the **Idea Friendly Method.** There are just three parts:

Gather Your Crowd with an idea that entices others.

Build Connections to turn your crowd into a powerful network.

Take Small Steps to accomplish your idea together.

It doesn't have to be any more complicated than that. This framework helps communities like yours break free from the "slow down and ask more questions" trap that keeps good ideas from happening.

I've tested it over the past 10 years, working with dozens of rural communities. This is part of the way Webster City, Iowa, recovered from the loss of a major manufacturer, filled 10 empty buildings, became their own heroes and saved their movie theater. How rural communities across the USA, Canada and globally are nurturing tiny businesses, expanding libraries, launching arts programs, and beautifying their towns. Not through grand plans and big committees, but through lots of people taking small, meaningful steps together.

Your community is next. Instead of trying to prevent failure through endless discussion, you learn by doing small tests. Instead of depending on a few leaders to decide everything, you involve lots of people in meaningful ways. Instead of discounting the ways you already do something good, you know that you are already making a difference. Instead of planning everything perfectly before you start, you take action and adapt as you learn.

Here's how we'll do it. In the first chapter, we'll walk through a complete example. Then we'll explore each part of the method in depth, with examples and how to make each part work in your community. Then we'll dive into the behaviors you need to make this stick as a lasting change. Finally, we'll apply this method in different situations, from working with skeptics to transforming organizations to collaborating across groups.

How Abby used the Idea Friendly Method and got her movie theater

Think back to Abby and her movie theater idea, when that adult told her not to even try. The secret that Abby knew and the adult didn't, was the Idea Friendly Method. She and her friends had heard my colleague Deb Brown and me present it at a conference.

Abby and the other teens said, "Let's make a temporary movie theater." The teens borrowed the school auditorium, picked a kids movie, and invited the grade school students to be the audience. Abby and the other teens ran the tickets, concessions, and projection. For one day, they created a real indoor sit-down movie theater experience for those little kids, an experience those teens wished they could have had when they were kids.

They **gathered their crowd** by working with other teen volunteers and their group advisors.

They **built connections** with the school to borrow the space and with the drive-in theater owner to learn about movie projection.

They **took a small step** with a movie showing that provided an amazing experience for one group of kids.

And that's the secret of being Idea Friendly: you don't have to listen when others say your idea won't work.

Write it down: Begin with your idea

Think of an idea you have for your community right now. Not what you think you should want as part of your job, necessarily. What really gets at your heart?

Think about how you'd finish these sentences:

IF our town had...

- an indoor movie theater

- a thriving downtown

- more ways for neighbors to connect

- *your own idea*

Or, IF our town was...

- a hub for the arts

- supporting young entrepreneurs

- welcoming new residents

- *your own idea*

Write that down now, before we go any further. One word, or one sentence.

Reading this on paper? Grab a pen and a notebook, or scribble in the margins. Reading the ebook? Highlight and add a note, or make a note on your phone. Listening with audio? Hit pause and open your notes app. Driving or have your hands full? Use voice dictation to record a note, or just say your idea out loud so you remember it. Then write it down when you can.

Whatever method you use, capture your idea right now.

That idea you just wrote down or said out loud? You have everything you need to start making it happen. You just may not know it yet.

You don't need permission, perfect conditions, or even full community buy-in. You just need the willingness to take one small step.

The pages ahead will show you exactly how, with real examples from communities just like yours. You'll learn how regular people and officials are reshaping their towns one small step at a time.

You can transform your community by taking small steps, starting now, without waiting for permission, support or perfect conditions.

Welcome to the Idea Friendly way of building community. What you do next is up to you.

CHAPTER ONE

The Idea Friendly Method helps you be more open to new ideas

Gather Your Crowd, Build Connections, Take Small Steps

From Lindsey Beckworth: For about eight years, I owned a bakery in Sandersville, Georgia, the small town of about 5,000 where I grew up. I can testify to how frustrating it can be to try to bring new ideas to fruition when the good old boys in power are stuck in the old way of thinking. Reading about the Idea Friendly approach on your website put words to everything I felt during the years I had my bakery — I wish I had found SaveYour.Town sooner!

You just wrote down your idea. Maybe as you did, you felt that familiar mix of excitement and doubt. The excitement of possibility, but also that nagging voice asking "Could this actually work in my community?"

Lindsay felt that same combination, excited but frustrated. You know that frustration of having good ideas get stuck in the old way of thinking. You've felt the energy drain of watching your community's potential get buried under endless meetings and objections.

The Idea Friendly Method gives us the framework to put words to those feelings and, more importantly, a way forward.

Here's how one person used the Idea Friendly Method to step up to a big challenge in her community without being stopped by that doubt.

Tracey's town faced multiple challenges

Tracey Homan lives in Gordo, Alabama, population 3,500, about 25 miles west of Tuscaloosa. When she described her downtown to me, she painted a picture you might recognize, of mostly boarded up stores with building owners from out of town, or those who use the empty buildings for storage. Not very many active businesses to count: a small used bookstore, a flower shop, a pest control business, a thrift store, and a bank.

For 12 years, Tracey drove 45 minutes to her job on the other side of Tuscaloosa every workday. As her boss started talking about retiring, Tracey faced a decision about the next phase of her life. She started to spend that commute thinking about her future.

And she knew even bigger change was coming. Within just a few months, a new highway bypass would open and go around their town entirely.

I can imagine that facing news of a highway bypass, some people might hope it won't really affect their town much, or say that they don't have anything left to lose. Margie Warrell, an author and leadership consultant who grew up rural in the Australian bush, said that we discount or deny the cost of inaction and sticking with the status quo. We tell ourselves "It's not so bad" and convince ourselves that our circumstances will somehow just get better over time.

Tracey couldn't change whether the bypass would open, but she could choose how she would react or even anticipate it. And she acted as if doing nothing had real costs. Their world was changing.

Openness to new ideas makes the difference

The world is changing around all of us, and Iowa State University has been studying what characteristics help communities facing change. They followed 99 small towns for over 20 years. In that time, those towns experienced every kind of change you can name. Some lost a manufacturer, others gained a new business. Some lost a local school, some had big growth in their schools. Some were hit by natural disasters, others were not.

No matter what happened or didn't happen, the towns that came through it the best were the ones that were open to new ideas. Those were the towns that saw "better economic and demographic outcomes" no matter what change threw at them.

ISU Professor David Peters said, "They realize no one is coming to save their town. If their town was going to survive and have a future it was going to be up to them."

It's that openness to new ideas that boosts our resilience. But what does that openness look like? How do we make our towns—and ourselves—more open to new ideas?

Tracey started by searching around on Pinterest for ideas and reading our SaveYour.Town newsletters.

"That's where your newsletters gave me inspiration," she told me.

Changing key behaviors creates openness

The Idea Friendly Method doesn't mean *saying,* "We should be more open to new ideas!" Or worse—saying, *"You* should be open to new ideas!" It means *shifting key behaviors* toward openness.

Gather Your Crowd moves away from a few people deciding for everyone. When you start with an idea that entices others, you're immediately opening up participation. You're not asking people to join your committee; you're asking them to be part of something they care about.

Build Connections breaks down the isolation that breeds closed thinking. When people from different groups start talking to each other, we discover possibilities we never knew existed. Connections help us find the resources we need and give us more options.

Take Small Steps cuts down the fear of failure that kills new ideas. When the stakes are small, people are more willing to try. When we see small successes, we're willing to try bigger things. Small steps build confidence and momentum.

Together, these three parts create not just openness to new ideas, but a friendly welcome for them. Now, all ideas are good enough to test. It's that openness to new ideas that makes a town able to cope no matter what happens.

Tracey decided to try her ideas

As Tracey thought about her future and read about the Idea Friendly Method and noodled around on Pinterest, she put together possibilities. To get ahead of that bypass opening, she wanted to create a business that would draw people into town. She wanted to create a downtown business for people to teach classes, a learning community.

Your brain may immediately react with, "That's a risky move!" or "Where did she get funding?" or "Did she rent or buy her building?" That's why we need to listen to Margie Warrell again. She says we consistently under-estimate our ability to handle the consequences of taking risks. Worse, we often come up with "dire, dramatic worst-case scenario images" in our minds. Rather than assuming we would act quickly to head off problems if things started going off track, we imagine everything spiraling out of control while we passively stand by. This is the fear that keeps people from trying and makes them want to 'protect' others from failing.

Tracey chose not to passively stand by. By starting small, she was demonstrating exactly how capable she was of handling whatever came up. And by keeping her day job, she minimized the actual risks while she learned.

She opened the Learning Block Studio with a simple concept: teach lessons in what people wanted to learn. She was open to all kinds of subjects including art, music, dance, fitness, baton, and sewing. She also wanted to offer a Makers Market for people to sell their products in tiny spaces.

Tracey Gathered her Crowd to offer more

She didn't start by hiring multiple teachers as full-time employees. Instead, she found people right in her community who wanted to share their skills and set up a commission-based system. The more classes they introduced, the more money they made. This aligned everyone's interests, and teachers succeeded when students succeeded.

Her crowd included stay-at-home moms teaching art and music, college students teaching fitness and baton, and a recent graduate from the university dance team teaching dance. Since Tracey still had her day job, she found a retiree to run the office during the day.

"All these people live in our little community," Tracey noted.

Tracey showed what the Iowa State University researchers called "a willingness to try new ideas and accept failure."

Tracey Built Connections to create opportunities

Tracey didn't just gather people to her idea. She Built Connections that would help everyone succeed.

"By using what I have learned from you," she told me, "I have made my Learning Block a place where you can rent space to try out your business ideas and hopefully grow to open your own business in our town."

She was creating a platform for other people's entrepreneurial dreams. The dance teacher hoped to grow her classes and start her own studio. If that happened, the baton and fitness classes could expand into the dance space.

The studio had a large room that had been a pharmacy, so they turned that into rental space. Another person opened a snowball and ice cream business there. They even used the old drive-up window for walk-up customers.

"I hope they will grow enough where they will move on to their own building too," Tracey said. "Then I will use that space for the birthday parties that our art and dance teachers have started doing."

Each connection created new possibilities for everyone involved, as people met each other, exchanged ideas and brought their friends and family into the studio.

Tracey Took Small Steps to learn and build momentum

Every piece of Tracey's approach demonstrated the power of Taking Small Steps. She didn't quit her job to launch a business and expect it to immediately support her. She didn't seek major funding or city approval. She didn't wait for a perfect plan.

She tested her idea with what she had, learned what worked, then adapted and expanded.

"This has been so exciting to watch play out," she told me. "People start sharing ideas and new ideas start building. Our customers and students come up with ideas making it so much fun. Our motto is 'We want to teach what you want to learn.'"

When officials don't show interest, keep going

Not everyone was immediately enthusiastic. This didn't stop Tracey.

"We haven't had much interest from our town government," Tracey admitted.

I've seen this pattern, and so have you. Remember Margie Warrell's research: when people (town officials, for example) are considering change, they often deny the cost of inaction and sticking with the status quo. Maybe you've felt this way yourself, when it felt safer to stick with familiar approaches rather than risk supporting something new.

But Tracey wasn't discouraged.

"They will come around to our way of doing business," she said confidently, "only because they want to know what people are talking about. We will win them over!!"

Tracey had created what the Iowa State researchers identified in thriving communities: "projects led by members of the community" with "a focus on projects that impact people's daily lives." Learning Block Studio met real needs while Tracey experimented her way forward.

The complete method in action

Looking at Tracey's journey, you can see all three parts of the Idea Friendly Method working together.

She Gathered Her Crowd with an idea that enticed teachers wanting to share their skills, students wanting to learn, and entrepreneurs wanting to test their business ideas.

She Built Connections by creating a place where everyone could help each other succeed. Teachers could build their classes, entrepreneurs could test their concepts, and the community gained a vibrant learning space.

She Took Small Steps by keeping her day job while testing, starting with what she had, and adapting as she learned what worked.

The three parts reinforced each other. Her crowd helped her build more connections. Those connections led to new small steps. Each small step attracted more crowd and created more connections.

Open behaviors create open minds

The Learning Block Studio fostered a community that was open to new ideas. Not through mission statements or strategic plans, but through specific behaviors that welcomed new possibilities.

The hidden benefit is how this changes the other people in the community who see it happening. Sometimes you have to see someone else starting something in order to be ready to take a first step on your own dream or idea.

"All ideas are good enough to test," could be Learning Block Studio's unofficial motto. Dance classes? Let's try it. Birthday parties? Let's test that too. Snowball stand in the old pharmacy? Why not!

Your turn to apply the Idea Friendly Method

You don't have to wait for your whole community to become more open to new ideas. Like Tracey, you can start by changing your own approach and creating something where others can join you.

To get there, you might need to overcome the same psychological barriers that affect all of us. Margie Warrell suggests asking yourself: "How will inaction cost me one year from now if I do nothing?" and "Where is my fear of failure causing me to over-estimate the size of risk and under-estimate myself?"

When you catch yourself worrying "Will this work?" ask "How could we test this?"

If anyone says "We don't have the resources," ask "What do we need for just the next small step?"

Rather than try to get permission, ask "What's the smallest version of this we could try right now?"

This shift in how you approach ideas—your own and others'—begins to create the openness that thriving communities share. You'll attract the crowd, build the connections, and take the steps that transform communities.

The method works because people like Tracey actually try it. And now you're ready to try it too.

Have you written down your idea?

Look back at what you wrote in the introduction. What do you want most for your community?

Now let's start applying the Idea Friendly Method to it:

- How could you test this idea in a small way?

- What would you need for just the next small step?

- What's the smallest version you could try right now?

Write that down now.

In the next three chapters, we're going to turn that idea into action using the three parts of the Idea Friendly Method.

We'll start by showing you how to Gather Your Crowd with an idea that entices others to join you.

CHAPTER TWO

Gather Your Crowd with an idea that entices others

You Gather your Crowd with a big idea, one that excites people and makes them think they can play a role in it.

You have your idea written down. Now comes the crucial question: How do you move from having just the idea to having a crowd of people excited to be part of making it happen?

There are as many ways to gather your crowd as there are people with ideas. You saw how Tracey gathered teachers and students around learning by creating a space for them. A different community gathered around sharing their ideas, and that kicked off more than a decade of positive energy and progress. We're headed to Akron, Iowa, population 1,500 people.

Share what you have to gather your crowd

My colleague Deb Brown worked with Akron in 2017. During her four days there, she spent time with people from all over the community to hear what they had to say about their town.

She even went to the old guys who drank coffee together every day in the former hospital building. Like many coffee groups, they had their complaints about the town, nothing huge. But one complaint stood out as completely different: They wanted to know why the town wasn't taking advantage of their workspace.

Turns out, these guys did more than drink coffee. They had created the Old Geezer's Club, actually a shared workshop. Here's how that happened. These guys loved woodworking, and they each had their tools in their garages. Makes sense, but it doesn't build much community. They had to go to each other's houses to see what they were working on or to do anything together.

Eventually, the wives told the guys to get all their darn woodworking equipment out of the garages where it was taking up space. The guys were talking that over while drinking coffee in the former hospital building. Someone pointed out there was work space in the basement they could use. That's where they moved their woodworking tools. Almost as a bonus, they could now work on projects together, or just hang around with each other while working.

But they didn't want to keep it to themselves. They wanted anyone in town to come and do woodworking using their tools. If you needed help or just company, they would come and help. They simply asked that you be careful and "don't do anything stupid." No charge.

These guys had gathered their crowd around what they could offer: skills, tools, workspace, and mentorship. We'll check back in with them a little later to see how they got more people involved.

Picture the usual public input meeting

Besides the Old Geezers, Deb met and talked to what felt like everyone in town, asking what they wanted for their community. Deb is really good at turning that question into excitement for the possibilities. Akron's next step was to gather that excitement by getting people together as a group to share all their ideas.

You can picture what that usually looks like: a big meeting room where people discuss ideas at tables, then share them to the whole group. Some people are assigned to capture all the ideas on big pads of paper and stick them up for everyone to see. Then everyone gets sticky dots so they can vote on their favorite ideas. Finally, someone gets assigned to write up the results as a plan. And that's the public input! I hesitate to think how many of these I've been part of over the years.

That is not what Deb and Mayor Sharon Frerichs did. They threw a party.

It's easier to gather with a party than a meeting

Everyone was invited. Not just the usual suspects, like organization leaders or business owners. Everyone.

They used a "Plant Your Flag" format. Anyone with ideas or a topic of interest like "youth activities" could write them on paper flags, then post them on their table. People could gather around the topic flags that excited them. Instead of focusing on problems, they focused on possibilities. Instead of asking "What's wrong?" they asked "What could we create?"

The atmosphere was completely different than those usual public input and sticky-dot-voting sessions, or the discouraging open meeting gripe-and-complain format. People were excited to share what they dreamed about for their town.

The mayor and some of the city council were there, but not as officials representing the city. They were there as resources to answer questions and make connections. They didn't come to decide which ideas were worthy or to control the conversation. They came to help.

No one needed to take notes for the group. Each person could write down anything important to them. No decisions needed to be made as a group. Each person could choose what they were motivated enough to do. These are key behaviors to shift towards being Idea Friendly, and you'll learn more about how to make these shifts in Chapter 5.

More people will join than start

Think back to the old way we used to do community engagement. The next step would be to form committees around each topic, have them decide on goals and subgoals, and set deadlines for accountability. Then each committee would meet and plan their specific action steps assigned to people by name. Maybe if we're really ambitious, we could put all the committees' plans into a combined community plan and timeline.

Akron didn't form committees. They just let people work on the parts they were excited about in the way that worked for them.

The first project to launch from the Idea Party was "Scooping the Loop." Young people got excited about recreating the classic car cruise by driving Main Street and hanging out downtown like people did in the 60s.

Seriously, do we need a committee to let people revive Scoop the Loop?

We just need someone to get it started, because more people will join than start.

Author Clay Shirky said, "The number of people who are willing to start something is smaller, much smaller, than the number of people who are willing to contribute once someone else starts something."

You've seen this happen over and over. Once someone kicks off a cool idea, others will come out of the woodwork to join. People won't come out of the woodwork for a typical committee project because they've already been burned out by that approach. Trust that there are people out there who want to join in when you start something meaningful that they can be part of.

Shift away from committee assignments

Do you even need committees at all, for anything? Maybe, but probably not nearly as much as you think.

The Stayton Sublimity Chamber of Commerce in Oregon killed off their committee structure entirely. Instead they gathered people only when needed for a specific project or activity. Elaina Turpin, former director of the chamber, told me they spent more time telling people how they make a difference in the community.

"Then your organization becomes a movement that people can get behind, not just another volunteer opportunity," Elaina said.

There's a difference between "please sign up for a committee" and becoming a movement that people can get behind. And that difference is being Idea Friendly.

Shift toward fun activities

This shift is already happening, especially with younger people.

When I was in Caldwell, Kansas population 1,000, I asked everyone in the room to introduce themselves. I noticed that the older people introduced themselves by the organizations they belong to and serve. One person said, "I'm on the alumni board, I volunteer with the historical society, and I'm on the executive committee for Vision Caldwell."

The younger people introduced themselves by the activities they enjoy doing. One younger person introduced herself a little uncertainly because she wasn't sure what to list. She said, "I like to garden. Um, some friends and I do a book club. Oh, and I have a Little Free Library."

She didn't list committees and organizations. She didn't belong to those, and she didn't define herself that way. She listed activities that she enjoys doing.

You apply this when you shift toward using activities to Gather Your Crowd. You'll entice the people excited enough to take action. People who are willing to pitch in, even in small ways, are much more valuable than any number of people who are just serving on a committee because it was pinned on them.

The Idea Party kicked off a movement that people could get behind

The flags at Akron's Idea Party included fine arts, youth activities, industrial growth, the old care center facility, park projects, and the swimming pool. Each group brainstormed together, and a lot of great ideas came up. They talked about how to create more places to eat locally, places for people to stay when visiting town, and how to replace the old swimming pool.

Even during the party, people started taking action by sending text messages and reaching out to others.

One of the ideas was new entrance and exit signs for the community. Remember the Old Geezers' Club and their woodworking tools? When they found out about the need for new signage at the edge of town, they were on it. They helped make the new signs.

In fact, those older guys started being more active in the community. They started working with the shop teacher and students at the high school. They have helped locals try their hand at woodworking before investing in expensive equipment of their own.

They even decided to change their name to be more open to new friends. Now it's the Down Under Club since they're still in the basement.

Mayor Sharon keeps sending Deb updates, many relating back to the Idea Party. After five years, they had seven businesses serving food, from the convenience store to a new corner bar with a remodeled kitchen to the old bowling alley with pasta nights run by a chef who moved from Chicago. The campground expanded to serve more overnight visitors and added a laundry and coffee shop. The community succeeded in replacing the old swimming pool with a new aquatic center that attracted an anonymous $250,000 donation.

Over time, leadership has naturally evolved. Sharon is now the former mayor. The Development Council leaders now include "a bunch of new, younger guys."

So much of the positive energy came from that visit where Deb asked everyone what they wanted for their community, and then Sharon threw an Idea Party with 25 excited community members.

Sharon said, "This is the best money we could have paid to open the eyes of various groups. Deb has a way of getting people in the community to get out and do something, and not just sit on our rears and hope something would happen."

How to Gather Your Crowd with your idea

You've seen how the people in Akron gathered around possibilities. Now let's look at practical ways you can do this with your idea, following someone who made it look simple.

Right after one of my talks, Heidi Johnson (Tymko) excitedly told me that she just realized she had been using the Idea Friendly Method, even though she didn't know it at the time. When she moved to a new small town in Saskatchewan, she wanted to meet new people. Her idea was to start a running club.

Share your excitement first. Heidi announced publicly that she was starting a friendly running club. She didn't try to get it all organized before sharing it because she just wanted to meet people through running.

Share what you're passionate about, not what committee needs volunteers. Spend more time talking about what could be, less time trying to plan the details ahead of time.

Share where people already gather. Heidi made her public announcement with a simple Facebook post that a running club was starting. She didn't create a complete website or formal organization.

Start where people are. For online, start with Facebook, especially local groups. You can go to other online places if it makes sense for you. For face-to-face, go where people already gather like coffee shops, groups, clubs, and other meetings where you're already connected. Or go old school, write letters to the editor, post on bulletin boards, and hang flyers around. For fun events, hold your own Idea Party, or set up a table or booth at an existing event.

Create activity at the location. Instead of meeting in a conference room or coffee shop to talk about running, Heidi suggested they meet and actually run together. Her Facebook announcement said "Here's a local route we could do" but then she added she was open to figuring out better routes together since she was new in town.

Do your gathering right at the location where your idea will happen. Get out of the meeting room.

Make it easy to say yes. Heidi didn't ask people to pay annual dues and commit to running every week for a year. She offered a simple online form to sign up for just one easy run/walk to meet each other.

Start with low-commitment ways for people to test their interest.

Let people start where they are. Heidi is a very long-distance runner, but she didn't make her running club about getting her intense workouts. She kept in mind that this was about building connections with her new community. She made sure to say that the club activities were easy run/walks so everyone could participate at their own level. Heidi didn't gatekeep the running club by demanding everyone match her pace or commitment level.

This is just like what Akron's mayor and council members did. They didn't expect all the ideas to fit into the town's strategic plan. They volunteered as individuals to help on ideas they loved personally.

Know that different people have different levels of ability and different levels of motivation. They all have gifts to share with the group.

Write it down: How will you gather your crowd?

Look back at that idea you wrote down. How can you put your idea out there to draw people to you?

How can you start with your excitement and share it where people already gather? How can you make it easy for people to say yes to trying it once? What activity could you do at the actual location? And how can you be a resource for others' participation instead of gatekeeping or over-organizing based on your own standards?

Write that down.

Let's kick this off right now. Send a text to your best friend who does everything with you, or post on Facebook to make a simple announcement that something is starting. Or fire off an email inviting someone to coffee and conversation. Do that now before you go on.

CHAPTER THREE

Build Connections to turn your crowd into a powerful network

Ask two powerful questions to expand your network and uncover resources

You've gathered people around your idea, now it's time to make it into a powerful network. A crowd can show up to an event. A network can make things happen.

The difference is connections, connecting people to each other and to the resources they need to succeed.

Just sharing the idea isn't enough

Picture yourself at the activity you just wrote down to Gather Your Crowd. You're at the site, there's great energy, and lots of people turned out. You're talking to someone who seems like a perfect partner for your big idea.

You know how these conversations usually go: you share your idea, the person nods enthusiastically and says "I hope you can make that happen!" Then they walk away and... nothing. They don't take any action to help.

There you are, left doing it all. Again.

They didn't mean to strand you. Most people want to support good community projects, but they don't immediately see realistic ways they can contribute.

Two powerful questions that change everything

Here are two questions that will transform lukewarm supporters into active helpers. Write these down or put them in your notes on your phone. Then you'll have them ready to ask everyone you talk to about your idea:

1. **"Who do you know who knows more about this?"**

2. **"Do you have or know where to find [specific resource] we need more of?"**

These questions work because they give people concrete ways to help immediately, even if it's small. Busy people know lots of people, so they can make an introduction. Someone may not have money to donate, but maybe they have access to another resource or connection. A person with mobility challenges may be your biggest cheerleader online. (Hello to Miss Dazey, one of our original online supporters!)

The beauty of these connection-building questions is that they lead to immediate action. Most people will do something small right away if they can.

Meet in-person to build sustained connections

Deb Brown experienced this kind of connection building when she lived in Hampton, Iowa, population 4,300. She joined a small group that included the owners of a couple of specialty shops, a flower shop, the winery, and Deb as a marketer. Some were new in business, and some had been at it for years.

They found out they had challenges in common: finding customers, getting customers to come back, marketing at events outside the area, and figuring out how to work together.

They decided to get together regularly. No agenda, no formal lectures. They answered each other's questions as best they could. By the end of each evening, they usually came up with some practical steps they could try together. And they did those. They kept meeting as long as it was helping them.

Without realizing it, they were asking specific versions of the two powerful questions constantly: "Who knows more about marketing outside our area?" "Do you know other businesses who have solved this problem?" "Where can we find out how to do a loyalty program for repeat customers?" "Where could I find some portable display shelves?"

The specialty shop owners already belonged to a broader business group, and they took some of the ideas to that larger network. One small group's connections multiplied across the whole business community.

Connection-based learning works better

Educational philosopher John Dewey said that adults do not learn from experience. We learn the most from *reflecting* on our experiences.

This explains why the Hampton business group's informal approach worked so well. Instead of attending formal small business trainings with fourteen-point outlines, they shared real challenges and reflected on each other's experiences. They got answers to their most pressing questions—the things keeping them up at night—rather than generic business advice.

This kind of support naturally develops into practical help. Maybe someone needs to learn QuickBooks and another person says, "Come over

Saturday, I'll show you the basics." Some of the best learning comes from someone who sits down and says, "Let me show you how to do that."

Go digital for lightweight connection building

You don't need formal meetings to build powerful connections. Alena Jennings runs The Doodle Academy, an art experience business in downtown Ponca City, Oklahoma, population 24,000. She connected with several other women who have retail arts and event-based businesses downtown to support each other.

They started a text message group to share with each other about books they're reading, things they're learning, events they're doing, and other ideas. When someone needs something, they ask the group. You can imagine the conversations: "Where can we find a guitarist for this weekend?" "Do you know any people who run food trucks?"

This immediate, convenient approach keeps the connections alive, whether they hold any in-person gatherings or not.

Make everyone a connector with these same questions

Once people start connecting you with others, teach those new people the same two 'who do you know' and 'where can we find' questions. Soon you'll have your whole crowd building connections.

You're accomplishing multiple things by teaching those questions:

- The whole group identifies more local resources and expertise

- People feel more invested and relevant

- You create a support team that can tackle challenges alongside you

Instead of you trying to figure everything out alone, you build a network where everyone contributes what they can.

Build Connections into your existing events

Gary Miller with the Elevate Douglas County partnership in Georgia has added connection building into the events they're already doing.

Before every business ribbon cutting, they ask what activities and causes the people of the new company are interested in. Then they find the related organizations and people from across the community—people who would normally never attend—and bring them to the ribbon cutting.

He and his colleagues spend time introducing and connecting people at the welcome ceremony. They also follow up afterward, bridging the new business owners into the community.

Gary is essentially asking the two powerful questions in a systematic way:

- "What causes matter to you?" (discovering their interests and potential resources)

- "Who works with [cause] around here?" (building specific connections)

Then he uses something he was already going to do—the ribbon cutting—to help those connections happen naturally.

The Old Way traps people into asking the wrong questions

Now that you have these powerful questions to use, let's look at how the traditional methods compare. Take Jessaca, an economic developer in Idaho who told me she's dying to get a microbrewery in her community.

Imagine if Jessaca had tried the old committee approach. She brings her idea up at her economic development board meeting: "I think we need a microbrewery in this town."

You can guess the questions the board would ask, can't you? "Who's going to run it?" "Didn't we do a market study 10 years ago?" "What makes you think it would work after that sports bar failed?" "What about liability?"

Do you recognize this pattern? These sound like questions, but they hit like brick walls. The Old Way traps everyone in the meeting room into focusing on objections and obstacles in order to be "responsible."

Gather people informally instead of in committees

Compare that to the connection-building approach: What if Jessaca started a homebrew group instead? She could bring together people who like to brew their own beer at home. Maybe hold a meetup in someone's backyard. They can share recipes, taste brews and compare notes. After a few beers, someone in that group is going to say, "I could run a microbrewery!"

Now instead of one person trying to figure it all out alone, or facing all the brick wall questions from some committee, they've built connections first. They have supportive homebrewers asking those key questions: "Who knows more about craft brewery regulations?" "Where can we find commercial brewing equipment?" "Do you know anyone who runs a microbrewery we can talk to?"

Same idea, different approach. They'll waste less time trying to find ways to overcome objections because they're spending more time building connections.

Connections boost the chance of success

Think about how much more likely that homebrewer would be to succeed now that they have supporters. They'd have built-in taste testers, volunteer help, suppliers identified through the network, and a group of people personally invested in their success.

That's the power of building connections first. You're not just talking to people or networking—you're creating the support system that makes success more likely.

This works for any community project. Whether you're starting an arts festival, improving a park, creating youth programs, or revitalizing downtown, the two powerful questions help you build the network that can make it happen.

Write it down: How will you Build Connections?

Look back at that idea you're working on. You have an idea for an activity to help you Gather Your Crowd. That's a perfect place to ask your two powerful questions to build connections around it:

- "Who do you know who knows more about [this topic]?"

- "Do you have or know where to find [specific resource] we need more of?"

Where could you create the equivalent of a backyard homebrew gathering for your community project?

Can you adjust your activity to get people together at the site of your idea instead of in a meeting room?

Write down your first steps for building connections around your idea.

Now reach out to one specific person who could help Build Connections ahead of your activity. Send a text or an email right now. Either set a time to grab coffee together, or ask your first version of "Do you know where to find [thing we need]?"

CHAPTER FOUR

Take Small Steps to accomplish your idea together

You and your newly powerful network accomplish the big idea by taking small steps

You're excited about your idea. You can picture how it could work. You've even found a few people who think it's a great idea, too.

Then other people hit you with barriers: "First you need to hold a series of community meetings, discussions and votes to drive people toward a shared vision of what success looks like, assign people to committees, discuss and vote on actions, then draw up the complete plan, then we can go for nonprofit status, and hopefully next year you can start the real work."

You feel that familiar energy drain. What started as an exciting possibility now feels like months of meetings and paperwork before you can even try one small test.

This well-meaning advice has trapped communities in endless preparation instead of action. While you're busy getting everything "right," your excitement fades, your crowd disperses, and opportunities pass by.

Instead, you can start right now with something tiny.

Small Steps let you learn more with less risk

By keeping tests and trials very small and immediate, we reduce the cost of failure to almost nothing. Author Clay Shirky said, "Failure is free, high-quality research, offering direct evidence of what works and what doesn't."

When we do a small test, we learn from it, then try a bigger test. Those small steps start building up to something greater. Rather than trying to do something giant all in one planned leap, we climb up to it, one step, one test at a time.

Authors Chip and Dan Heath said that good solutions are strikingly smaller than the problem to be solved. So don't worry that you're not doing enough, or that small steps don't matter. Small steps are how we get traction against those big, complicated problems our communities face.

Small steps mean we waste less time talking and spend more time doing and quickly learning. We're getting action more quickly, and we're visible in the community more quickly. People can see we're taking action, and then more people can be drawn to us.

Starting small builds more benefits than waiting to do something big eventually

In Tionesta, Pennsylvania, population 500, a fire destroyed a block of storefronts in their downtown. Their local economic development group spent 10 years responsibly looking for a developer to rebuild this block of buildings and getting turned down by everyone. Meanwhile, those empty lots sat there contributing nothing to the community.

Then they came up with a smaller idea. What if they put storage sheds or little garden sheds on the lot? It would be a temporary space for smaller businesses, a facilitator for pop-up businesses. And then if they eventually secured a developer, they could move the sheds.

They bought sheds, then found a local carpenter to add old-timey false fronts to make them look like mini-downtown buildings. They did such a good job making it feel like a part of the downtown that it encouraged building owners across the street to improve their storefronts and facades.

It's called the Market Village, and the tiny businesses draw locals and tourists into the downtown. Other businesses now stay open later hours to match the evening hours of the Market Village. It has helped people launch tiny businesses into larger spaces and others to contribute even if they don't have a lot of financial resources or perfect health. The rural winery and the bakery from a neighboring town opened tiny outlets here. The businesses help to market each other with great events, like the kids' art festival.

Julia McCray was on that original economic development group. She said, "Artisans are selling their products; tourists are coming to see 'the Village'; residents and seasonal residents are coming back to the downtown; a couple of the shops have hired part-time help. This project shows that 'pop-ups' work and are good for a community!"

After 10 years, Tionesta Market Village is still thriving.

Starting small now yields bigger benefits than waiting to do the big thing eventually because of trajectory. Science educator Steve Maier put it this way, **"Significant change will occur with minimal force if applied over an extended period of time."** Your small steps are that minimal force applied over time.

Tionesta succeeded in turning an empty lot into an economic draw because they were open to the new idea of trying something smaller right now.

Write it down: Your first small step

Look back at your If Our Town big idea.

- What tiny test would get you closer to the idea?

- How could this connect with your activity on the site where you'll gather your crowd and build connections?

- What minimal force can you apply now to create significant change over time?

Write that down now.

When you look at it, what you just wrote down probably still feels big. That's a holdover from how you've been trained to think and work. Stick with me for one more story of how to think smaller but keep it meaningful.

Give people small but meaningful ways to participate

When I first visited Pullman, Washington, population 30,000, they had a dirty sidewalk problem. Every time it rained, dirt and leaves and stuff washed out of the streets and onto the sidewalks. They said they'd like to have a welcoming and clean downtown to draw people in.

After we walked around downtown, we brought the group together to talk about next steps. A few people talked about doing another cleanup day, but no one spoke up to take it on. One guy tried to pin it on the chamber director, so she reluctantly picked up her pen to write it down. You've seen that pattern before: guilting someone into saying they'll do it, almost blaming them for not having done enough.

I stopped that. I said, "If no one here wants to take the lead, then it won't happen because it isn't your own priority." We sat for a while longer, and I think people were pretty uncomfortable.

Then Willow, a business owner, put up her hand and said, "I'll clean up my sidewalk." Perfect! I said to take pictures, put it on social media.

Hashtag it #CleanYourOwnSidewalkDay, and ask everyone to join in. Every time you clean your sidewalk, keep posting it and tagging it. Make a big deal out of how everyone can do their own sidewalk, too.

It's better to have one person willingly take one tiny action than to force more work onto someone or an organization.

Consensus emerges from action

Consensus won't come from voting on what most people want, or trying to compromise until the majority of people can reluctantly agree. If we had taken a vote in Pullman, most of them would have voted for a clean up day, even though none of them actually wanted to do it.

Consensus emerges from the actions people are motivated enough to take. The whole group might not go the direction you personally would want, but when you start gathering your crowd, you pick the direction you go. The people who want to do that too will come with you.

When I was back in Pullman, seven years later, Willow still kept her own sidewalk and storefronts clean. She told me that Clean Your Own Sidewalk Day in Pullman was Wednesday, and the city sent around the big street sweeper machine that night. Locals built on that momentum to schedule some more cleanup days to pick up the common areas. The momentum had slowed in the past couple of years, and that's natural. When my colleague Deb was there the next year, Pullman had replaced and widened a bunch of the buckled and damaged sidewalks. Several businesses have refreshed their fronts with sitting areas and planter boxes. Will this restart Clean Your Own Sidewalk Day? It might!

Attract, not convince people who are initially reluctant

This is your best way to attract those people who are initially resistant. If Willow had tried to convince everyone during the walkaround or at that meeting to change their minds, forget doing a cleanup day and all sweep their own sidewalks instead, and also to convince the city to change their work schedule, everyone would have resisted. "That will never work!" "That's a terrible idea!"

Willow didn't try to change their minds. Instead, Willow attracted them by taking her own action. She made it easy to join in. Willow started a movement that people could get behind.

I used to run a retail store myself. I won't be going to any public meeting to talk about how we need to be a cleaner community. I won't sign up to serve on the beautification committee for a year. I may or may not turn out for that Clean Up Day you organized. But if you tag me on social media and say it's Clean Your Own Sidewalk Day, I'll get my broom.

Write It down: Your meaningful steps to attract others

Look back at the small steps you thought of, connecting your activity at the site to gather your crowd and build connections. How could you make your next step smaller, but more meaningful?

- What's the smallest version you could do on your own or with one friend, right now?

- How could you make it visible so others see it happening?

- What would you hashtag it or call it so others could join?

Write that down now. And then do it.

- Take your first step on your own, take pics and post it online. Tag two friends

- Or text two friends to join you on the first time. Each of you take pics and post it online, each tagging two more people.

Do it now.

CHAPTER FIVE

New behaviors, tiny tests and immediate action make change easier

The Idea Friendly way is the easy way

From Stephanie Ray, Stillwater County, Montana: The Idea Friendly Method helped our small team remove the barriers that events require committees, multiple meetings, and multiple levels of decisions. We took our idea, divided up a handful of start up tasks, and hit GO. When we round tabled our results, we were all shocked that 75% of the event was done and what remained was manageable. Our team was also pleasantly surprised at how many people popped out of the woodwork to help once they saw the momentum of the event. I'll continue to use the Idea Friendly Method more and more with the hope it carries forward to others.

***

You've thought of your small steps, and you're ready to take action. As you build on your excitement, let's make sure you don't slip back into old patterns.

Stephanie's experience captures where you are right now. You've seen how the Idea Friendly Method works, you want to keep using it, and you want to spread it to others. But knowing something and making it stick are two different things.

It's normal to slip back into old habits

Even when we know better, it's easy to fall back into familiar patterns.

From Deb Brown, Webster City, Iowa: This one was hard for me to picture how it would work. Even when I was thinking in an Idea-Friendly way, I envisioned Gathering Your Crowd as bringing everyone together in one space. Then someone would take notes, and someone would put ideas up on the board. Then you told me no one has to be the secretary and take notes, and everyone writes down what is important to them to act on. And there might not even be a gathering! **Once I accepted this as something that could be done, I was all in. I realized then that Idea Friendly was different, and it was going to change the world.**

Even Deb, who was my collaborator and first tester of the method, found herself defaulting to old committee-style thinking. That's normal. We've been trained in and used these patterns for years.

Remember your real goal: community, not efficiency

When you feel yourself slipping back, remember this:

The goal of old way behaviors is efficiency. The goal of Idea Friendly behaviors is community.

When you're tempted to streamline, control, or avoid "duplication of effort," ask yourself: Am I prioritizing efficiency or community right now?

Community building will look messy or inefficient from the outside, but it creates the social connections that make everything else possible. When community is your goal, the behavioral choices become clearer.

Five behaviors that make idea friendly stick

Here are five specific behaviors that help you build lasting Idea Friendly patterns. Each one naturally moves you away from old patterns toward new ones.

Behavior 1: Get out of the meeting room

This builds the pattern of being informal instead of formal.

City hall or county chambers or the boardroom just feel oppressive. Have you noticed that? The whole formality and weight of the past can make you frown as soon as you step inside! I swear that negativity has seeped into the walls in some places.

If you're having a meeting about anything to do with downtown, wouldn't it make sense to do that where you can look around and actually see the downtown?

The location affects the conversation. Sitting in the council chambers or a meeting room, you're too far removed from the life and activity you're trying to create. Sitting outside downtown, you get a chance to be part of the scene and to think about the potential for improvements.

Behavior 2: Be conspicuous doing your thing in public

This builds the pattern of being connected instead of isolated.

Doing something out in the real world where people can see you shows a level of commitment. And it's even better if you are not alone doing it.

Nothing draws a crowd like a crowd.

Make people slow down to get a look. Make them curious. Get people to stop and ask what the heck you think you're doing. Then you have a chance to share a bit about your big idea, and the small but meaningful way they could be part of it right now.

If you've ever had someone say "I wanted to believe in your idea, but I just couldn't see it," this is why you want to be conspicuous doing things in public. Create experiences for people to get a better sense of the idea.

Behavior 3: Do cheap tests that approximate your idea

This builds the pattern of testing instead of deciding.

No matter what your big idea is, there is a cheap way to do something at least sort of like it to generate attention. Each time you're involving more people (Gathering Your Crowd), letting people talk to each other in a friendlier setting (Building Connections), and you're giving everyone a small but meaningful way to participate (Take Small Steps). You're helping people see your idea so they can believe it's possible.

Here are a few quick examples of how to test an idea cheaply.

Want to start an ice cream parlor? Go buy some ice cream bars and popsicles. Make little stickers for them with your hashtag or a way to contact you. Set up a table in an empty lot and give away a few ice cream bars on a warm afternoon. Hand them out to people along with notes telling them about your big idea.

Wish you could get more support for murals? Let's make some murals with chalk. Divide up the downtown, and let lots of people create chalk murals in all the blank spaces. You get lots of people involved, and you can try lots of different art styles and ideas. After a couple of rains, it just washes away!

Considering changes to sidewalks or streetscapes? Mock up the potential improvements in the actual downtown. Mark proposed ramps with duct tape. Borrow potted plants to stand in for proposed plantings. Where you want to add bricks, draw a brick pattern with sidewalk chalk. Then invite everyone downtown to walk through it. Watch to see how the plans hold up in the real world. What works? What doesn't? Listen for people's ideas and comments.

Behavior 4: Do just a tiny part of your idea now

This builds the pattern of small instead of big.

Doing a tiny part helps everyone see how possible it is. You'll learn from little failures and small successes. It's so easy to try something tiny, there's no need to wait while we get all the pieces together before starting. We can check our results instead of guessing and writing detailed formal plans.

Want some examples? Here you go:

Dreaming of a community dinner that closes down Main Street? You can start with two card tables on the sidewalk and just a few friends. Then invite more friends next time, and keep growing until you're shutting down main street.

Wish downtown was clean year round? Remember Pullman's Clean Your Own Sidewalk Day. One building owner started the year-round movement just by sweeping her own sidewalk and inviting others to sweep their own.

Wanting to start your own business? Holyoke Hummus Company started with a small folding table at a local park selling falafel sandwiches.

Soon they went mobile with a little push cart. When they outgrew the cart, they bought a food truck. Now they're scaling up commercial production.

Behavior 5: Build the community first

This builds the pattern of involving the crowd instead of relying on a few people.

When I first considered starting a shared coworking space in my hometown of Alva, Oklahoma, I talked with Derrick Parkhurst who helped start a successful space in Oklahoma City. He told me to build the community first, the community of people who would want to use the space. It was the best advice that I didn't follow. My co-working space didn't last long, mostly because I didn't have a community of people who wanted to use it.

You can "build community first" for any community building or shared space. Do meetups and events, borrow existing spaces, or use empty lots. Get people together doing the thing they'd do in the building. Then when the building opens, you have the community ready to move right into it.

Idea Friendly behaviors bring extra benefits

You'll get more help when you go informal instead of formal.

Deb discovered this when Webster City, Iowa, wanted to add holiday lights downtown. The first year, she was Chamber of Commerce director, so she used the formal approach: Deb called the city manager, who assigned city crews, and they put up lights. The only role for everyone else in the community was to come look at the lights.

A few years later, Deb was "just a volunteer" and tried the informal Idea Friendly way. She posted on Facebook that everyone was welcome to help wrap trees at 1 pm Saturday. When she met a new acupuncturist in town, she asked him to join. The mayor came with his two grown sons. Someone brought a ladder. A store owner said "I'll do the tree in front of my store." It was an hour and a half of pure community building and fun. The trees were lit, and a lot more people were allowed to play a meaningful role.

You'll save time when you get out of the meeting room.

Toni Henry told me how the East Brady, Pennsylvania, Beautification Group members were having trouble finding time to both attend meetings and do beautification activities.

Toni said: I always said they came to meetings to eat cake because refreshments were always provided! But when asked if they could show up on another day to weed the park, they were busy. I assumed they used up their available hour meeting and eating cake!! So I suggested that instead we meet at the park with tools, and while we are weeding we could 'meet.' After weeding we could stop at the Old Bank Deli for ice cream, supporting a local business. That seemed to work!!

Toni discovered that getting out of the meeting room and being conspicuous doing the work in public actually saved time and got better participation, even in a town of 800 people.

You'll create better events when you involve the crowd instead of controlling everything.

Stop planning events all the way out. It's often enough to create the context for people, such as a summer arts festival downtown. Set broad guidelines to clarify what's allowed, like keep it family friendly, no alcohol.

With the context and guidelines set, people will come up with ideas you never would have thought of, like human foosball. When you involve the crowd in creating the event, they become creatively invested in its success.

You don't plan every detail because the event isn't your real goal. Community is your goal.

Download this behavior change infographic

For a complete comparison of old way vs. Idea Friendly behaviors that you can share with others in your community, download our free infographic. It's perfect for showing to people who persist in old habits: "See, right here, it says 'test, don't decide.'"

It's available on the book resource page: saveyour.town/IFGuideResources

Write it down: Change your approach to your idea

Which one of these five behaviors leaps out at you? Will one change how you approach your big idea? Is there one you kinda hated that's telling you something?

Write that down now. Then take action now with a small way to practice that behavior today.

- Get out of the meeting room: Text someone to meet you at the actual location instead of an office

- Be conspicuous: Post a photo of yourself doing something related to your idea

- Do a cheap test: Try the smallest possible version of one element

- Do just a tiny part: Take one small action toward your bigger goal

- Build community first: Hold a meetup of the people who would be involved in the big idea

Take action right now.

CHAPTER SIX

You can't lose people who were never yours

Spend more time Gathering Your Crowd than trying to convince skeptics

From Mary Ellen Coumerilh, Goodland, Kansas: We opened a shave ice and coffee house on our declining Main Street because we realized Main Street is the heart of any rural community and our town's heart was broken. Your resources have been a huge help in our efforts to build community, not only with our customers but also build a neighborhood of Main Street businesses. For us as a Main Street eatery, I have to say that we have been embraced for the most part by the old guard, as we've been at it for 5 years now and refused to worry about what others think in terms of being part of the approved group. I think that our Main Street is now over the hump, a lot because I've taken your advice on being Idea Friendly and just kind of did the stuff whether or not I've had the chance official imprimatur so to speak.

***

You've learned the Idea Friendly Method, you're trying new behaviors, and you've already taken your first actions. And you will run into people who resist your approach or criticize your efforts. It will happen. But there is one thing you need to know:

Those are not your people. You can't lose people who were never yours.

Spend more time Gathering Your Crowd than trying to convince old-way organizations

Paul Thompson from a small town in Ontario (population 8,000) learned this lesson the same way we all have to. He spent considerable time trying to get community organizations and officials to implement economic initiatives he felt their community needed.

Finally, he decided to give up on trying to convince them.

Paul said, "So I am using your advice and shifting to talking to other business owners directly (via private Facebook group for now) and planting the seeds of some of your ideas for sidestepping the bureaucracy and just trying some stuff ourselves."

Paul discovered that you can't lose people who were never yours, even when those "people" represent entire organizations that should be helping.

Instead of continuing to fight institutional resistance, Paul found his actual people: other business owners who wanted to take action. The town already had a successful Sunday morning market, so Paul was inspired when some newcomers started a cultural night market. They bypassed all the old conflict and insularity by creating something new rather than trying to reform what already existed.

As Paul put it: "The old 'easier to ask for forgiveness than permission' approach, as far as is practical. There's a strong mindset among many that the Town/Chamber etc. should organise/run these and the businesses will participate, so there will be a lot of work to shift the mindset back to personal agency."

Paul shifted from trying to convince resistant institutions to empowering people who were ready to take responsibility for their own success.

Don't try to convince individual critics, either

This principle applies to individuals, too. Deb Brown discovered this when she was chamber director in Webster City, Iowa. There was a retired chamber member who came to every event and always ate a lot of food. He was a grouchy sort, Deb said. One year they had a big event set up next to his house. He stormed out and started giving an event volunteer grief, and demanded, "Who planned this? That damn Deb Brown?!"

Deb said she continued to speak to him politely, but she realized he was never really "hers." Despite coming to every event for years, he wasn't open to her ideas.

"That Damn Deb Brown" practically became Deb's tagline. She even put it on a t-shirt. And it taught her that you can't lose people who were never genuinely with you to begin with.

Some people prioritize being in control over building community

These resistance patterns don't always mean that someone hates you or your idea. They may be prioritizing control and perfection over community building. You probably won't hear them put it in those words, but there are a lot of "control enthusiasts" out there.

I heard from one volunteer who said, "I put my heart into volunteering for a special event only to be ripped apart for how I made the coffee." Ouch.

That's far from an isolated incident. People have shared dozens of stories like this with me. One local church volunteer tried to help serve the meal after a funeral, and got told off because she cut the pickles the wrong way.

It's not supposed to be about the pickles. A bereavement meal is intended to allow a family to grieve together and to receive a gift from their church community, and it allows people in the church community to share their gifts with a family who needs them.

When people get stuck on "doing it right" instead of "serving the community," don't try to convince them. Those are not your people.

You cannot lose people who were never yours.

Put your efforts into building a stronger community.

You build a stronger community through experiences that bring people together from across different groups to each play a meaningful role

Those efforts you put into building a stronger community can also reduce the amount of resistance you'll run into, if you do them in this specific way.

You build a stronger community through experiences that bring people together from across different groups to each play a meaningful role.

You need to notice three key parts of that.

Experiences give people something to reflect on. Adults learn not by doing, but by reflecting on what we have done. Reflecting on experiences offers opportunities for people to learn and change old behaviors and attitudes, and ultimately reshape their values in a positive way.

Bringing people together across different groups helps get past bitter dividing lines. When we do something that a member of the community might do, we start to see ourselves as members of the community. We develop a new identity.

Each person playing a meaningful role makes the experience our own. We were part of it, so we care more about it.

When all three parts come together, you're changing the way people see themselves, the way they think and the way they act within your community.

This helps people feel relevant. At a Dakota Resources virtual coffee meeting, gerontologist Leacy Brown said when people don't feel relevant anymore, they can behave in ways that aren't positive or helpful. She suggested finding ways to help them be meaningful participants, even if they're not in charge.

Leacy was talking about older adults, but can't you see this applying to everyone? Don't we all want to feel relevant?

It will take more than one experience to help someone feel relevant and willing to consider new ideas. They need repeated chances to experience something and then reflect on that experience. It's like how you varnish a piece of wood: one thin layer at a time.

You'll get those thin layers of experience and reflection when you make more projects into community building opportunities. As long as it includes all three parts, it adds up: it's a new experience, it brings people together across groups, and it gives everyone a small but meaningful role.

That's the Idea Friendly Method.

You Gather Your Crowd for shared experiences.

You Build Connections between people across different groups.

And you give everyone a small but meaningful role to Take Small Steps.

This is your best way to overcome opposition. Not by force, but by enticing.

Don't wait for everyone to get on board

Take positive action with the people who are ready. Create those experiences that bring people together across groups to each play a meaningful role. Let the results speak for themselves.

The people who were never really yours will either come around when they see success, or they won't. Either way, you'll have built something meaningful with the people who were genuinely interested.

You can't lose people who were never yours, but you can find the ones who are.

Write it down: Pick one positive action

Think about your idea and the people around you. Instead of focusing on who might resist, ask yourself these two questions:

What's one positive action I can take this week that brings people together across different groups to each play a meaningful role?

Are there existing successes that I could build on rather than trying to reform resistant institutions?

Write that down now.

Now take that action.

CHAPTER SEVEN

Attract positive people with activities they'll enjoy

Entice others without over-organizing

From Jaime Shanks, Glendive, Montana: We recently formed a group after [learning the Idea Friendly Method at the] ReImagine Rural sessions - very loose group that is more about action vs. meetings. We call ourselves the "Vigiplantes" (based on vigilantes but we are planting new ideas, beautification, actual trees and plants). We may do stuff at 2am to surprise people the next morning. We're making beautification fun and visible!

***

You've learned not to waste energy on people who aren't yours. Now let's focus on attracting the ones who *are*.

It's up to you to find positive people to Gather Your Crowd. The negativity wants to take over if you don't have positivity to cancel it out. You can transform your community by taking small steps, starting now, without waiting for permission, support, or perfect conditions. That doesn't mean you have to be alone.

Attract people with positive energy

When you put positive statements where others can see them, you give positive people a reason to be part of your ideas. Whether you post online, in person or in the media, you're enticing positive people to join you.

Use the Creed as a hook

The Creed is that thing at the beginning of this book, the one that starts "We are a community of possibilities, not of problems." When you share it, you'll be attracting the kind of positive people you most want to connect with. You can download it at:

IdeaFriendly.com

Print it out, add your community's name and hang it up. You can also share it online. Feel free to post it far and wide.

One reader reacted to the creed with this thought: "Beautiful! I'm a board member of The Sister Cities of Franklin and Williamson County in Franklin, Tennessee, and I think this is the best expression of what we're about."

Create your own Success List

Carol Peterson from Milnor, North Dakota, has kept a huge list of all progress from new businesses to public improvements for 12 years now.

Carol told me: I continually hear from community members (the naysayers) that we don't ever get anywhere, we are at a dead-end. Milnor is a city of under 700 people and yes, you may think we are not going anywhere, but I have the ammunition to counter these people with my data. We have 25 businesses today that we did not have 12 years ago... Can you believe that Milnor has received over $2.3 million in grants since 2010!

Imagine the next time someone says, "There's never any new businesses here." And you're ready with your success list. Or the next "Nothing good ever happens in this town" post on Facebook, and Carol can reply with 25 new businesses in 12 years and $2.3 million in grants. I would be posting that list on every social channel, reprinting it in newsletters, and tacking it up on the cafe notice boards.

"Hi, welcome to Milnor! Here's a copy of our success list!" could be the best way to welcome visitors and potential new residents, if you ask me.

You can see Carol's list at this book's resource page, and the link is in the last chapter.

Here's why success lists work: We can learn from what worked before (my friend Rob Hatch calls that "success frames"). Instead of a nebulous "nothing good" mindset, you have specific things to point to and examples you can build on.

Everyone likes to be part of something that is working. That makes a success list a great tool to Gather Your Crowd.

Look for people and groups who already act Idea Friendly

There are people and groups already using Idea Friendly approaches in your community. You just need to know how to spot them.

Look for newer groups already acting Idea Friendly. Like Gettysburg in Action in South Dakota, which does bike-a-thons, 5K races, holiday events, craft shows, children's plays and concerts.

Kara told me: They communicate via their cell phones and social media. A couple of the gals are coordinators and handle the money that is raised but the group is so organized/unorganized. They are able to figure out who can handle what event and who needs to do what. Your webinar made me realize how GIA is getting it and should be the model for our other and older organizations.

That "organized/unorganized" description is perfect. They have just enough structure to function, but enough flexibility for people to contribute in their own way. And Kara's recognition that this could be "the model for our other and older organizations" shows exactly what you're looking for: groups that naturally work the Idea Friendly way.

Look for innovative business owners who share opportunity with others. Rose Williamson of the Crow Reservation in Montana started her beaded jewelry business from her home, then expanded into making clothing. She sells at pop-ups, in person events around the state, and online. Because Rose is fairly well known now, she gets a lot of invitations to larger events, and she doesn't always go alone. She often reaches out to other, less well known artists to come with her and exhibit their art. She has been able to spread opportunities to more Crow artists to sell their products at places like the Big Sky Indigenous Women Fashion Gala and Art Market in Billings.

Rose embodies the Idea Friendly approach: she started small, built connections, and now uses her success to help others take their own small steps.

Create your own positive action groups

What if you made your own informal positive action group? It's easier to start a new positive group than to breathe life back into a dying old organization tied up with bureaucracy.

Community happens when people talk to each other. When we talk to each other while creating something together, we strengthen our community ties.

Take inspiration from these informal action groups:

Stealth Gardeners, in Southampton, Ontario (population 3600), come out between 8pm and midnight in the summer to water sad potted plants, pull weeds, and spread mulch in public flower beds. They divide overgrown hosta plants into smaller plants they can offer and donate to neighborhood plant sales. Most townspeople never see them, but they have a lot of fun and inspire others to remember to water and pick up trash.

Sublette 365, in Sublette, Illinois (population 370) is a group of young professionals. They picked that name because they know they can do something positive for their community every single day.

Ninja Power-Washers in Cold Spring, Minnesota (population 4300) started as lunch conversations. Deb asked some young people if anyone had a power washer. One woman said "yes, and I love it!" When Deb explained what it means to be a ninja (show up and do something nice), everyone at the table got excited about cleaning up streets and doorways. They leapt into action that same day.

Why these groups work so well

Notice how these groups work more like viral crazes than traditional committees. People can participate in one short burst (like ninja power-washing) without committing to year-long service. This appeals to how younger people want to engage: they'd rather grab a broom when they see it online than join the beautification committee.

Old way committees are like old social media: centered on existing personal connections. This is the hidden reason old volunteering keeps coming back to the same ten people.

Your new way is centered around activities and experiences. Think about how your projects could be more like challenges or crazes. How could people be involved just for the short term? What if all people had to do was participate in one short burst and share the results?

Go regional for even more support

You can take this to the next level by reaching out to positive people in your region. Attend regional and national conferences, and start your own "Idea Friendly" get together. Come a little early or stay a bit late, maybe grab a meal together. But make an ironclad rule that this is a positive group. It's a great place to talk about the Idea Friendly method. You'll keep each other's enthusiasm going. Send me pictures so I can cheer you on!

Write it down: Start your own positive action group

Right now, send a text to someone who will be the first to join you. Then block a time on your calendar for the first meetup. You don't need it all planned out, just pick a person and a time and begin.

If you need something for the group to talk about, use our SaveYour. Town videos to hold watch parties. Or use Deb's colorful workbook, Save Your Small Town, as a book club for action. Links to these are at this book's resource page:

saveyour.town/IFGuideResources

The key is to start with positive energy and make it fun. Like the Vigi-plantes say: make it about action, not meetings.

CHAPTER EIGHT

Don't worry about permission or approval

99% of the best things you can do don't require anyone's permission

You've gathered positive people around your idea and you're ready to take action. Now someone's going to say, "But is that legal?" or "Don't you need permission for that?"

Stop right there.

99% of the best things you can do for your community don't require anyone's permission.

Most good ideas don't need permission

When I presented at the Oregon Mid-Valley Rural Conference, the code enforcement expert spoke right after me. Right at the beginning of his talk, he looked straight at me and said, "Every one of your Innovative Rural Business Models is illegal!"

I just grinned, nodded and agreed!

The code enforcement guy went on to talk to the entire audience for an hour about how outdated rules and codes hold small towns back. He hammered them with how they can and should adopt new ones. Clearly, he understands that illegal today doesn't mean illegal forever. It doesn't mean you can't *ever* do it.

Don't let an outdated law or rule stop a great idea for your community. Ask why (and when) that rule was first adopted. Then talk through all the things that have changed since that day. Maybe it's time to change it.

If they won't change the rules, start with what you *can* do. Deb and I keep a list of over 100 great things you can do without anyone's permission. You can guess what we call it: 99% of the best things you can do for your community don't require anyone's permission.

Here are 10 meaningful small steps from that list that don't cost much, don't need permission, and are important to your community:

1. Hang out downtown, in the park, in plazas and pocket parks. Take a book or a snack. Invite friends. Have conversations.

2. Spend more time in your front yard and on your front porch.

3. Take pictures of things you like in your town and share them online.

4. Start a rock hunt. Find some small rocks, paint them and hide them outdoors downtown. Make a hashtag or online group so people can post photos when they find them.

5. Sweep your own sidewalk.

6. Carry a small trash bag when you walk or run to pick up trash.

7. Create chalk art on sidewalks, bare walls, and retaining walls.

8. Tell a traditional story or ghost story to young people.

9. Add positivity to online groups. Volunteer to moderate com-

ments.

10. Make a "What to do in (our town)" Pinterest board.

Which one will you do right away? Can you text a friend to join you?

Go get that full list right now at the book resource page, and feel free to spread it around your community:

saveyour.town/IFGuideResources

When they say your idea is illegal, you have options

Asking officials for approval is a terrible way to try to start an untested idea. They don't know if it will work—yet. Why would they say yes?

When faced with a new idea and request for permission, officials and sometimes others may quote a rule or regulation that seems to make your idea illegal or out of bounds. People have tried to label all kinds of cool ideas as illegal: selling from booths on sidewalks, operating food trucks on public streets, painting crosswalks with fun designs, and selling a few handcrafts without a business license.

So start smaller, in a way that doesn't require permission—yet.

When someone tells you that you can't do something, here are your five best options:

Option 1: Walk away and do something better.

Stop beating your head against the wall. Go find some better way to build community. 99% of the best things you can do for your community don't require anyone else's permission.

It's hard to walk away from an idea you love, I know. Think about the goal that's behind your idea. Because it's almost always not about the idea itself. It's about shaping your town into the kind of place you want to live. And fighting with the rule-makers is not the way you want to live.

Option 2: Go smaller - Take Small Steps.

Take a good look at your idea. Are there any small steps you could take first, that may not be illegal? Maybe you want to have a Food Truck Festival but your code says no selling of food from parking spaces on Main Street. To start smaller, you could invite just one or two trucks to come and set up in the parking lot behind a store.

When you do a smaller version of your idea, track the results. For the food trucks, did people come and eat from the food trucks? Did the nearby stores see more customers? Were the restaurants still busy? Now you have some results of your test. You can take those results back to city council and ask for permission to try it again, this time on the Main street.

Option 3: Read carefully to find a legal alternative.

This is my favorite way to deal with accusations of *"illegal!"* Out-think them to find a "just legal enough" solution.

Lots of towns have old "no selling on the streets" rules. Fine. We'll sell on the sidewalk, in a private parking lot, from an empty lot or in an empty building. Or maybe we won't "sell" at all. Maybe we'll give things away for free, and maybe get a sponsor to donate and cover the cost.

In one town, volunteers wanted to try a farmers market in a town park. The local government said they'd need to provide insurance and to follow additional regulations on what could be sold. The volunteers could have stopped there, but instead they spent some time searching the rules. Armed with a new alternative, they moved the event to the downtown sidewalks and called it a Street Bazaar. Turns out, different rules applied on the sidewalks than in the park, and "bazaars" were treated differently than "farmers markets." No need for insurance or limits on what vendors can sell.

See? Just legal enough!

Option 4: Be subtle and don't draw too much attention.

There are a lot of ways to do something that's good, but possibly *not quite* allowed, without making a big deal of it.

Deb was in Paulding, Ohio (population 3500), and noticed an ad for a local gym painted on the side of a vacant building. When she asked locals about it, they told her that gym was no longer in business. Deb asked one of the guys if he had any paint. He said he could get some. Deb suggested they go Saturday morning, paint over that sign and put up their local hashtag, #MyPaulding.

He said "what about the laws?" Deb asked him if he knew what laws those might be. He didn't. He did know that the building owner lived in China and was unlikely to come back.

The building was empty, and the outdated sign was misleading. It made sense to take a positive action.

Notice that Deb didn't start by saying the council should get involved, or that they should send an official letter to the owner. Just be subtle.

They met on Saturday. He painted over the sign and put up the hashtag while Deb held the ladder and waved to people driving by. One was a city council person. One was the sheriff who waved back. A few folks who walked by loved the idea and said it was about time someone got rid of that outdated sign. Everyone was curious. And no one found any rules that were broken.

Option 5: Pay the fine and do it anyway.

Want to know a big secret? Lots of small town fine schedules were set up decades ago and are actually quite small amounts. If that's the case, why not go ahead and pay it? Call it a permit fee after the fact.

If the fine is too high to pay yourself, try taking up a collection from other like-minded folks so you can pay the fine and do it anyway. If lots of people think the idea is good enough to pay part of the fine, then that's good evidence to the council that the old rule no longer serves the community.

Use the Idea Friendly Method to make it happen

Even when dealing with permission issues, you can use the three-part method. (You knew I'd say that.)

Gather Your Crowd around your big idea. Put it out there and let people come to you who think it's a good idea. You're looking for people who are enthusiastic and positive, not more rule-enforcers.

Build Connections with people in other towns to gather examples. Connect with your council of government or other regional groups for even more resources and connections. Connect with donors or supporters. And remember that your councils are actually good connectors. They know lots of people who can serve as resources.

Take Small Steps by trying smaller versions of your idea that don't require anyone's permission. Do pop-ups and other temporary things that don't trigger rules. And remember that conversations are still free! Community happens when people talk to each other, so that's a great small step.

Write it down: What you can do today

Look at that list of 10 things that don't require permission, then check the online list of over 100 ideas. Pick one you can do this week. Or think about your big idea: what's the smallest version of it that doesn't require anyone's permission?

Write that down now, then go do it.

Remember: You have everything you need to start.

CHAPTER NINE

Revitalize organizations by cutting formality

Groups can adapt by being open to new ideas

From Kathryn Witherington, Walla Walla, Washington: Truly cannot say enough about the Idea Friendly method for this - I've used it in the last 6 years to create two downtown public spaces, including millions in investment from the city, and am now using it to grow affordable housing opportunities.

***

Once you practice the Idea Friendly Method as an individual, you can apply it inside of organizations. Local chambers, nonprofits, clubs, and volunteer groups can get bogged down in rules and negativity. Being open to new ideas can revitalize older formal organizations. The Idea Friendly Method gives specific new ways to change how we do things together.

If you're part of one of these voluntary organizations, you have a choice that government officials don't have: You can choose to abandon structures that aren't working.

Don't worry, officials, we've got your back in the next chapter.

The time has passed for old organizational models

Carol Coletta, a civic and public space expert, said: The time has passed when a few influential people could gather in a room to decide what a city will be. Instead, a city's future is determined by hundreds of actions taken daily by thousands of people based on what they believe about a city's future and their role in it.

If this is true for cities with all their legal constraints, it's even more true for voluntary organizations. Your chamber, nonprofit, or community group doesn't need to cling to outdated committee structures from the 1850s.

Those organizational charts and formal committee systems were created to take advantage of the communications tools available in the mid-1800s: the telegraph and typewriter. Today we each carry super-communications tools that put those to shame. We can quickly broadcast to a crowd, easily communicate back and forth in groups, and instantly connect with individuals.

Replace committees with talent pools

We're going to replace those outdated committee systems with a more modern talent pool model. Don't just rename "committees" to "talent pools" without changing how they work.

Committees are formed and hang around for at least a year, maybe forever. They meet regularly, someone takes notes, and someone gets to be in charge. Why do we act like the meeting is the important part? The *action* is the important part.

A talent pool could form at any time, for any length of time as needed. When a project is finished, the talent pool can dissolve or reform. You don't *call a meeting* of the talent pool; you *call on* people from the talent pool as needed. Sometimes you have individual contributors working on their own, sometimes teams working together. Team members may change over time, whether a year is up or not.

Kathryn Witherington says the Idea Friendly Method has rewritten her perfectionist brain. She told me about working on an affordable housing project in Walla Walla, Washington (population 32,000). When she met a person who volunteered their talent with legal titles and property transfer issues, she wanted to rethink the ways that person can share those important skills. Let that person be in a talent pool instead of on a committee. They contribute when their skills are needed, then they're free to move on to different things.

Let people just try their ideas

Even if your organization might seem to be "in charge" of something, it can still allow people to just try their ideas without any further interference.

Deborah Mansfield moved to West Point, Mississippi (population 9500), and she wanted to paint a mural. She went to the Main Street organization's design committee.

"I'm an artist," she said. "I want to paint a mural on a wall downtown. What do I have to do to do it?" She was expecting the usual formal process: submit several proposed designs, wait for review by the committee, then maybe voting by the public, all with no guarantee her design would be chosen or approved.

Instead the Main Street person said, "Talk to the building owner."

That was all it took. Deborah painted her mural.

Create it together: Tale of two concerts

To highlight the difference between old organizational thinking and Idea Friendly approaches, let's look at the tale of two small town concerts.

Concert 1: We've done all the work, you just need to show up.

This concert happened at an agritourism business in Oklahoma. They brought in a couple of professional musicians for performances out at the farm. The musicians were pretty well known, and they had been on TV shows you've probably heard of. But audience turnout wasn't that great, and a friend of the owner pointed out the conundrum in a post online:

"People keep saying there's nothing to do in this town, but when we do put on something special, they don't turn out."

I'm sure you've run into this, too. You work hard on events and things to do, then only a tiny crowd shows up. It's frustrating!

This is the Old Way: a few people in control creating a performance event. They decide what the concert will be, with an emphasis on big names, then if there isn't a big crowd, it's a failure.

Concert 2: Let's build it together!

The second concert happened in Iowa. A young man of about 25 named Mike walked into Deb's office at the chamber of commerce. He said he wanted to have more live music in town. Could she make that happen? No, she said, but he could.

With some encouragement, Mike picked a night, and Deb helped him get permission to use the stage in the park downtown. Then Mike went out and gathered his crowd. He found local musicians who would play. He talked to all his friends. They spread the word, so more people heard about it. Those other people spread the word, too, and Deb helped spread the word through the chamber.

They kept talking about the concert as a group effort, and that they were open to ideas and help. People figured out what they could do to participate. Some told everyone they knew on Facebook, others made posters, and one person suggested adding open mic time.

There were no committees, just people who wanted to hear music in the park. When the concert happened, lots of people showed up. Many people just listened, some sang at the open mic, some joined the jam session. A dance troupe performed between sets, and everyone had fun.

Even though it wasn't done by the usual formal organizational process, the Lions Club could include this event in their reports of activities because they sold dinner. The Chamber could share in the credit for helping organize and promote it. All without a single committee meeting.

Design the event then announce it vs. announce the idea and design it together

If you design the event then announce it, people's only choice is whether to attend or not. If you announce the idea and invite people to design it together, they can decide to attend, promote, invite others, contribute, join in, suggest new ideas, or create a whole new part of the event. Out of that list, they just might find a way to participate.

Organizations can stay relevant, participate meaningfully and get credit while empowering community members to lead. The Lions Club and the chamber didn't have to organize the whole concert. They just contributed what they do well.

It will be chaotic. You won't be in control. But you don't do events because you need something to control. You do events to build community.

Your organization can choose to transform

You can transform your organization by taking small steps, starting now, without waiting for permission, support or perfect conditions.

Kill off committee structures entirely. Create talent pools that form as needed for specific projects.

Let people test their ideas without endless committee review.

Co-create events *with* the community instead of creating events *for* the community.

Focus on empowering others rather than controlling outcomes.

Control isn't the goal. Community is the goal. And community happens when people work together in ways that feel natural and meaningful to them.

Write It down: How can you co-create with your community?

Think about your organization's next project or event. Instead of planning it all yourselves, how could you invite the community to create it with you? What would you need to let go of? What could you gain?

Write that down now.

Send a text or call that one person in the organization who is most likely to join you. Ask if they want to grab coffee and talk about a new way of approaching that next project.

If you can't think of anyone, that may be the sign you were waiting for. It's not fun to think of leaving, but maybe you'd be happier going back to Chapter 7 and starting your own positive group.

Chapter Ten

Officials and boards lead best by empowering others

Community is our goal

From Sharon Shewmake, State Senator from Washington: When I got elected, I thought it was my job to do cool stuff, and it turns out it's actually to empower other people to do cool stuff.

***

Compared to everyday folks, elected officials carry additional responsibilities and must follow more rules. You can still be more Idea Friendly and play a key role in making your community more open to new ideas.

If you think of your role as empowering other people to do cool stuff, you'll try to find out about as many new ideas as you can. You'll publicly ask people what new ideas they're working on. You get to encourage all of them, help them Build Connections from your extensive network of resources. And then invest your limited resources in the ideas that show promise as people test them.

Listen for new ideas in the community

Your easiest small step is to refocus how you listen to people. Listen for people who share the new ideas they want to work on, whether that's a new business, a new mural, or a new activity. Become resources for them, instead of just listening and not being able to act upon it.

The frustration of the old town halls, where it turns into a gripe session, comes from listening but never taking action. When you give your community a chance to share their ideas, encourage them all to take their own action. Be clear that you're there to answer questions to the best of your knowledge and share your connections to outside resources from your network.

You don't pick the winning ideas

Lots of ideas you'll hear will not be great. Some of them will fail—in fact most of them probably won't ever happen. And that's ok. You are not trying to pick winners. You want the people to test their ideas out, see if they work or not, then adjust and try again.

If you're tempted to tell people their ideas won't work, take a deep breath instead. Maybe they will fail, but maybe this is just the learning opportunity they need to apply to their next big idea. Or maybe they'll think of a way to do it that you wouldn't have.

Remember, it's not *you* that's testing the ideas out. You are listening for ideas, offering appropriate connections, then watching for successes as *other folks* try their own ideas by Taking Small Steps.

Clay Shirky says when we keep the experiments small, "Failure is high-quality research, offering direct evidence of what works and what doesn't."

The successful ideas might surprise you

Have you heard about a rock hunt? It's a simple idea: people paint some small rocks and hide them around town. Other people look for them, often families with kids looking together. When they find a rock, they post photos online. That's pretty much it. You might think it's silly or that no one will participate, but it's not your job to pick winners. You encourage all people to try their ideas, help if you can, and then see what happens.

Bolivar, Missouri, tried a rock hunt, and in 7 days they had 3000 people join their Facebook group. That's like the entire population of Bolivar.

The city administrator said in an interview, "If you set up 10 different things and said, 'Which of these things do you think will spark the community and take off,' I don't know if this is one I would have picked."

And that's the point. We *don't* know which one will work, so there is *no reason* to set up 10 different ideas and try to pick. Let all 10 people test their own idea.

Follow the Superior rules for town openness

Mayor Mila Besich of Superior, Arizona, shared their superior rules for how to be Idea Friendly while still complying with requirements. They didn't write these rules because they were already a perfectly happy town where everyone gets along and no one causes conflict. In fact, they were more like your town to begin with.

Mila reached out to me a few years ago, saying "Our community is small, 3,068 residents, less than two square miles. We have many challenges and have had all sorts of internal conflicts. We are an example of how any community can overcome those conflicts."

She shared their Top Ten rules on how they try to run things from inside Town Hall.

1. Always keep an open door and be willing to help individual citi-

zens solve their problems.

2. Support community giving organizations (nonprofits, clubs) through non-financial means, such as using the influence of Town leadership to support events.

3. Make town facilities available and optimized for community programs as cheaply as possible.

4. Participate in and honor the contributions of community organizations.

5. Always be willing to do what you can (within the rules) for your fellow man.

6. When you find an ordinance or policy that is unfair, don't be afraid to change it.

7. Look for ways you can work with other groups and individuals for positive change.

8. Be willing to take a back seat to others' ideas. Do not insist on complete control and be open to putting time and resources behind those ideas.

9. Insist that all code and zoning reviews are completed in a timely manner, with no backlogs or waiting lists. This makes expedited permits unnecessary.

10. Look for ways to say yes. Things that are impossible as written may be possible with a simple change of approach. Know the code well enough to be able to navigate the customer through that process.

Mila told me: We wanted to share some of our ideas with your readers on how we have stayed idea friendly. This is mostly an attitude and philosophy but has proven to be helpful for our success. Most importantly, don't be afraid to dream big and communicate as often as you can with everyone.

Any local government, including yours, could copy those 10 rules and start living by them. You don't have to be that "perfect" town to start this conversation. Remember, Superior used these rules to change attitudes and communicate with everyone staring during some pretty contentious times.

Design projects for public involvement (not just public input)

Open communication like Mila described extends to how we do public input. The old way of doing public input was holding meetings at city hall, often at times inconvenient for the public. The agendas were static and limited, and the whole process felt like we were enemies. Officials made the important decisions for the people and then told them.

The new way is to involve the people in the process of designing and even making decisions.

Urban design expert Mukul Malhotra said, "If you design a street, don't design it while sitting in a room. Go to people. Get design ideas from kids. And test. As designers we don't always know what will work."

It's not that experts and designers have no role. It's that the people deserve a bigger role in their own communities. And with today's technology and the Idea Friendly Method, they can have that role.

Get out of the meeting room, even if the project is moving a landfill

There's a town in Tennessee that needed to expand their current landfill or face dire consequences of escalating costs and even threats to their town's future. There was room to expand the landfill, but that land was being used as a park. Since the park was funded with some restricted funds, it couldn't just be taken over for landfill unless it was replaced with another park. Officials had a couple of possible new park sites in mind, but the public was up in arms over the loss of the old park.

Officials were saying, "We have to expand the landfill or our town will die!" And people in the community were saying, "You can't take away our beloved park for landfill!" You could imagine this kind of fight in your town.

What would an Idea Friendly approach look like?

Let's get out of the meeting room and go to one of the possible new locations for a park. We can pop-up a temporary park in one of those other locations. Let's have a picnic there for everyone. Let's pop-up some possible activities, like a pop-up splash pad, and bring outdoor toys and games.

While we have people out at the potential new park site, let's post some drawings of what it could look like if we moved the park here. Let's engage people in conversation about what this park could look like and what the consequences are for not expanding the landfill. And let's capture people's ideas and input.

You can just feel that this conversation is going to be much different from the shouting match in a traditional public meeting.

Now let's hold another picnic at another of the potential park locations. We could even do more than one at each site to reach as many people as possible.

Each time we're involving more people (Gathering Our Crowd), letting people talk to each other in a less combative setting (Building Connections), and we've given everyone a small but meaningful way to participate (Take Small Steps.)

"Including people in decision-making shouldn't be that revolutionary of an idea," Sarah Wilson, of the City of Birmingham, Alabama, said.

If we can make a landfill expansion into an Idea Friendly project that strengthens our community ties rather than strains them, then we can use the Idea Friendly method on any project. Even the one in your town.

Replacing that aging city pool starts with kiddie pools

City pools are a great example for Idea Friendly projects. Lots of small town pools have reached the end of their useful life, and many local governments are facing tough decisions.

If you need to replace your city pool, don't talk about that from the council chambers. Get a group of families together at the pool location. Ask them to bring their dollar store kiddie pools and water toys. Then while the kids are playing in the tiny pools, start conversations with the adults about ideas for the pool in a nonthreatening environment.

Someone is going to say, "That would have to be posted as a public meeting, it's not an approved accessible location, and you'd need liability insurance!" But that's all a dodge.

It doesn't have to be official. You don't have to be involved as officials or board members if you can empower people as community members to take initiative. Of course you'll post it as a public meeting if that will keep it legal. But let go of control. You're working towards an empowered community that would create a discussion like this spontaneously, on their own. And the whole community will be stronger for it.

Community is our goal

Too often, people tell you what your goals as an official should be. You should be more efficient. You should be thrifty with residents' money. You should hold staff to account.

Actually, community is your goal. That's why you do all the hard work, to improve the quality of life of your people. You don't have to battle this alone. All the groups, all the organizations, all the boards in your town—bottom line, they all care about quality of life. The definition of what makes better quality of life for your place comes from your people.

John Shepard is an expert on rural planning, as in the city planning profession.

"Quality of life should be a core planning principle," John said. "Quality isn't just 'pretty.' It matters because it reflects that we value where we work and live; that we value our friends and family every day."

It's easy to forget community when you're mired in debate on legal technicalities at a council meeting. You can forget when you're struggling to maintain an event that has been around for decades that's getting harder and harder to keep alive.

The event isn't our goal. The technicalities aren't our goal. Community is our goal.

So what if it isn't the best festival ever? So what if the flyers had some misspelled words on them? So what if someone said they'd do something, but they didn't get it done?

If you remember that your real goal is building a community, it becomes easier to accept the imperfections that make us human beings. We may not be doing it your way, the way we've always done it, or the way the rules say, but we are building community.

Efficiency isn't our goal. Compliance is not our goal. Community is our goal.

Your role is to empower others

Maybe you can't abandon all structures, but you can:

- Focus on empowering others rather than controlling outcomes

- Listen for new ideas and connect people to resources

- Design projects that involve people meaningfully, not just input sessions

- Look for ways to say yes within existing rules

- Allow others to take the lead on their own ideas while you provide support

- Remember that community is your goal

You can transform your community by taking small steps, starting now, within the constraints you face. Your role isn't to do cool stuff—it's to empower other people to do cool stuff.

Write it down: How can you empower others this week?

What's one way you can shift from controlling to empowering this week? How can you listen for new ideas and connect people to resources instead of making all the decisions yourself?

Can you print out the Superior Rules for Town Openness and post them (anonymously, if necessary)?

Write that down now. And take action right away.

CHAPTER ELEVEN

Bring groups together to find collaborators and spur new ideas

Build robust collaborations for meaningful purposes

From Cheyenne McGriff, Wall, South Dakota: The event was a success! About ten community members joined the meeting, shared their calendar and enjoyed coffee and conversation. This was a community need that is now filled. We look forward to more "Coffee and Calendar" events and continued community collaboration.

***

Whether you're leading an organization, serving as an official, or working as an individual with an idea, at some point you'll want to collaborate with others. Building on what you've learned to empower people around your ideas, it's time to connect across different groups to find collaborators and spur new ideas.

In rural communities, collaboration is both a natural act and a huge challenge.

Collaboration is a natural act because people represent multiple organizations. When just a few people work together, we can list all of those organizations as partners, and it sounds like a great collaboration! Really it is still just a few of us doing the work.

Collaboration is a huge challenge because we have to work with people still doing things the old way. Silos. Territorialism. Not wanting to step on other people's toes. People worry about duplication of effort or feel reluctant to take on something new that might be controversial or cause problems.

Often the best collaborations don't come from the people with the most important titles or serving in the highest elected offices. Instead the powerful collaborations come from regular people and the decisions they make every day about how they will work together to stretch their limited resources.

Think of this as a continuum from simple coordination, to active cooperation, to deep and meaningful collaboration. We'll look at three different ways to build your collaborations.

Start coordinating with Coffee and Calendars

You can't start collaborating when you don't even coordinate. Often local groups work on similar projects, but each in their own silo. Sometimes they're doing almost the same thing in completely different ways or in ways that conflict with each other. Of course, we have an Idea Friendly way to approach better coordination.

Try coffee and calendars. Here's how it works.

- Invite some people you'd like to coordinate activities with to coffee.

- Ask them to bring their organizations' calendars.

- Go somewhere together and get some coffee.

- Let someone from each group go over their calendar and tell what they have planned.

That's all. Just share coffee and calendars.

Then do it again later and invite more people. Maybe monthly will work for you, or maybe quarterly is better. Try it out and see.

You're not trying to convince them to change what they are doing. You are trying to entice them into cooperating by seeing opportunities for themselves. As each person reviews their calendar, others can gradually start talking about maybe cooperating or doing shared projects or noticing that they have shared goals. Entice, rather than convince.

Tip: Start with people and groups with similar interests

Start with anyone you want to build better coordination with, anyone who might be working on something even slightly related to your idea. Maybe ask members of local organizations, groups, clubs, the municipality, chamber of commerce, school board or groups, tribes, or county government.

Trap to avoid: Don't use this to make a combined community calendar

The goal isn't to make a combined calendar of all the community events. Do not try to replace the coffee time with an online calendar app. It's about the conversations and connecting people across the different groups. It's not about the calendar.

Start collaborating by making a list of who else cares about this

If you have some existing momentum for cooperation, you can take the next small step. From calendar sharing, you can move toward a specific collaboration.

Before I arrived for a working visit in Irvine, Kentucky (population 2,200), economic developer Joe Crawford reviewed some of their previous strategic plans. He was pleased when he found that without referring to those plans day by day, they had accomplished almost all of what they set out on paper.

Joe gathered the people he called the "core group +", the ones who helped write previous strategic plans for the county. He emailed me about what he wanted to do.

"These are the folks who are doing the most moving and shaking," Joe said. "I'm thinking giant sticky notes and addressing some of the big issues we're trying to tackle. This will be a great crew, so you'll be one of the homies, and we'll be picking your brain."

When we all got to the pizza place, I asked them **what challenges were so big that only this group could address them.** That set a larger goal than just picking my brain. Housing was one of the first challenges to be mentioned, but it didn't generate much immediate enthusiasm in the group. It seemed like it was too big of a challenge to fix, with no clear path toward progress.

I applied the Idea Friendly Method. First, you Gather Your Crowd. I stood next to one of those giant sticky notes and asked who all would be vitally interested in improving housing in the county. They could start with the organizations they belong to and serve, then see who else came to mind. Here's the list they came up with:

Cities, county; Housing authority; Local house flippers and rehabbers; Contractors; Real estate pros; Surveyors; Banks, appraisers, inspectors, lawyers, Legal Aid; Large employers; School district, tech center; Utility companies; Kenny (they all knew him); Hardware stores and lumber yards; Habitat for Humanity; and the development district.

Just making the list uncovered some assets they hadn't thought about. One suggestion led to another. Then, because they're experienced at planning and doing, they naturally started putting the pieces together, Building Connections

The city owns some houses that need to be rehabbed. The local tech center teaches building trades. They have several local building contractors. That led them to their initial idea: Experienced building contractors could work alongside building trades students to rehab a city owned house and get it ready for a new family.

Of course they thought of and addressed some initial obstacles. They'll need money, and with such a compelling project, they felt confident they could find funding to support it. The students aren't yet qualified to do everything that needs done, so the contractors will fill the gaps. Maybe the city wouldn't be able to participate for some reason, but they knew of a local company that owns an empty house that could be a likely target.

Focusing on one specific and small project instead of the huge goal of "we need more housing" kept them thinking about next steps instead of objections. They were also suddenly enthused and ready to work on it.

Trap to avoid: Don't write the plan

Here's what we didn't do: we didn't write this as a formal strategic plan. Instead, they started Taking Small Steps immediately. They knew enough to start reaching out to the tech center, the city, contractors and other key people. As for the rest, they can plan as they go, adding the details they learn, adapting and keeping the project organized without making it inflexible. And without adding another strategic plan to the shelf that they won't look at again until the next planning cycle.

This is the Idea Friendly Method. You start with your big idea for your community, the thing that you feel will improve your quality of life. Like, "Contractors mentoring students to rehab city-owned houses." You use that goal to Gather Your Crowd. Like setting up a text message group of the people who are interested at first. You turn your crowd into a powerful network by Building Connections. "Who knows the building trades instructor?" And you and your newly-powerful network accomplish that goal by lots of you Taking Small Steps. "I'll get a list of possible houses from the city."

Deepen collaboration and build robust networks for a targeted purpose

You're moving up from building coordination with Coffee and Calendars to building cooperation through asking "Who else cares about this?" The next level is deep, long-lasting collaboration.

Dell Gines from the International Economic Development Council (IEDC) described collaboration as "building robust networks for a targeted purpose." That one sentence is packed with meaning. *Build* starts with active effort. *Robust* has to be strong, not just casual. *Networks* are interconnected, not just one person driving it. *Targeted* focuses that intentional effort on something specific. *Purpose* brings it all together for deeper meaning, beyond just hitting a goal.

People have to connect as people before they can collaborate

In the late 1990s Curtis Wynn was hired as CEO of Roanoke Electric Cooperative in North Carolina. He said that the diverse communities the cooperative served were in "probably one of the most economically distressed regions in this nation" with 23% of the people living in poverty compared to 14% of the US population.

"These circumstances did not happen overnight, and we know that they're not going to be fixed overnight," Curtis said.

He felt the cooperative could play the role of catalyst to enhance the quality of life, and one tool available was the newly introduced federal Empowerment Zone program. That designation could yield around $40 million of tax credits, tax incentives and grants for their region.

Curtis said he reached out to everyday folks and key community stakeholders across four counties to work together to apply. Because the federal application process was complex, they started regular gatherings bringing together people from grassroots organizations, non-profits, local governments and community-based organizations to work on it.

They called it Roanoke Chowan Partners for Progress, and chose four common concerns that were quite broad including healthcare, education, financial literacy and common economic development. That put some bounds on the conversation so they didn't have to try to solve *all* the problems in *all* their communities at every gathering.

To help people connect across their differences, Curtis said they intentionally included a fellowship meal and informal time to talk with each other at every single gathering. That helped them feel connected as they learned more detail about their regional challenges, what each organization was doing and ways they could work together across divisions.

People have to connect as people before they can collaborate.

After almost a year of working together, they submitted their application. Unfortunately, they were not selected.

"That was unfortunate in some ways and fortunate in others," Curtis said. "After receiving the bad news, every stakeholder that was around the table agreed that the process that we used to get that application together was more important and more valuable than the funds would have been had we received the grant."

There were times when not a lot of people showed up, but they stuck it out. They stuck it out through the pandemic, meeting online. They are still working together, more than 20 years later. Together, this collaboration leveraged far more money than that one program could have offered them.

When you build a robust network for a larger purpose, it doesn't have to fizzle out if you miss one goal.

Apply this to your collaborations

Think about the idea you've been developing through this book. You've learned to Build Connections. Now you can use collaboration to amplify your impact:

For Individuals: Start with Coffee and Calendars to have conversations and learn all the great things others are doing.

For Organizations: Instead of trying to control partnerships, ask who else cares about this? Collaboration can emerge naturally.

For Officials: Use your convening power to bring groups together, but let them determine how to work together.

The goal isn't to eliminate all duplication or create perfect efficiency. The goal is to build the relationships that make everything else possible. Community is our goal.

Do it now: Start Coffee and Calendars

Take the first step by writing down two friends who would join you with their calendars. Send them a message right now to set up your first Coffee and Calendars gathering.

You don't need it all planned out. Just pick people, pick a time, and begin.

CHAPTER TWELVE

Stay open to new ideas to position your town for the future

You don't have to know all the answers if you stay open to new ideas

From Kathryn Witherington, Walla Walla, Washington: I am pretty much an Idea Friendly evangelist here in Southeast Washington, and we've seen really cool results in the downtown revitalization space, and now I'm loving exploring how to bring that same philosophy to affordable housing and other community work.

***

You've come a long way since you first read the Creed and wrote down your idea. You've learned to Gather Your Crowd, Build Connections, and Take Small Steps. You've discovered how to build habits that stick, focus on positive people, work without permission, and collaborate across groups.

But here's what's really happened: You've become someone who stays open to new ideas. And that positions both you and your community for whatever the future brings.

You don't have to know all the answers if you can be open to new ideas

You don't have to be an expert to start making your town more Idea Friendly. It doesn't matter how closed others are to new ideas. With every small step you take with just a few others, you'll be doing what Chip and Dan Heath called "acting our way into a new way of thinking."

Carnell Chosa, of Jemez Pueblo, co-founded The Leadership Institute at the Santa Fe Indian School to identify people in the Native American community who are open to new ideas. "I'm a bit of a preservationist," he said in an interview. "We realized that a community intellectual is somebody who is always moving the community forward with the changing times, changing resources and new ideas. Our lives are different because of our ancestors who themselves were always moving things forward for our communities."

You can be open to new ideas while staying connected to tradition. You can honor what came before while adapting to what's coming next.

Your community is different, so you have to test your ideas

Adapting to what's next means testing ideas for our own unique local circumstances. While we share some common challenges, the assets in a Maine fishing village and a remote Australian town and your town aren't all the same. That's why we test our ideas.

Even if you find an example where someone tried this idea in their town, it won't necessarily apply. Even if an expert tells you it will work for your town, that is just a starting point.

And we're not a mini version of big cities. Ideas that worked in some big city will need testing, too.

That's why the Iowa State University research matters so much. They studied 99 small towns for 20 years and found that regardless of what happened to them—whether they lost a manufacturer, gained new businesses, faced natural disasters, or experienced school changes—the towns that prospered best were the ones that stayed open to new ideas.

It's that openness to new ideas that makes a town able to cope no matter what happens.

How openness to new ideas creates community resilience

Kathryn Witherington can't help but talk about the Idea Friendly Method. As Executive Director at Common Roots Housing Trust in Walla Walla, Washington, she's seen firsthand how small, doable steps and a willingness to try things out can add up to big changes. Over the last six years, she's used this approach to create two downtown public spaces, attract millions in city investment, and now, to grow affordable housing opportunities.

Kathryn's journey started with downtown revitalization. When she took the lead on Walla Walla's Main Street in February 2020, no one could have predicted what came next. COVID hit, and suddenly, the rules changed. Restaurants couldn't serve indoors, so the community needed a new way to gather. Instead of waiting for a perfect plan or a committee's approval, Kathryn and her team took action. They shut down a street that already had string lights, added wine barrel flower pots, and set up tables, chairs, and umbrellas, purchased by the city with federal grant funds.

"If it fails, we can take it down in like a day," Kathryn recalls. That attitude of trying something, seeing what works, and being ready to adapt, became the foundation for everything that followed.

By the end of 2021, the city council was considering shutting down the outdoor space. But the community had already fallen in love with it. Out of 297 public comments, 204 were positive. If they'd started by trying to push it through the city council instead of testing the idea first, Kathryn says, "everyone would have been outraged." Instead, the success led to more permanent features and even city funds to convert parking spaces into platforms. They took out 32 parking spots, and people still come downtown.

What started as a COVID adaptation became proof that their community could create spaces they'd never had before. That's resilience: the ability to adapt and create solutions when faced with challenges.

Kathryn's latest challenge is housing. As part of Common Roots Housing Trust, she's working to build and sell homes at affordable prices while keeping the land in community ownership. She's using the Idea Friendly approach here, too, sometimes without even saying it out loud.

When people told her the model would never work because of skepticism, Kathryn said she already knew how to deal with skepticism because she knew the Idea Friendly Method.

"We can try, fail, and sell them off," Kathryn said. "Why *not* try it? No one has a comeback to that."

When your community develops this openness, you're not just solving today's problems. You're building the capacity to handle tomorrow's challenges, whatever they might be.

All ideas are good enough to test

Change your default answer to any new idea. Right now, most people's default answer to new ideas is to say no, ask a lot of questions or raise objections. Your new default answer is "What do you need to test that idea?"

This doesn't mean being reckless. It means being smart about learning. When we do small tests, we learn what works quickly and cheaply. When we don't test, we either miss opportunities or make expensive mistakes.

Author Margie Warrell asks the question we have to ask ourselves: "How will inaction cost us, one year from now?" What are the negative consequences of spinning our wheels, talking problems to death, and continuing to slow everything down?

While we're busy trying to avoid failure through endless discussion, the world is changing around us. The real choice isn't between being safe where we are and taking risk by changing. It's between the change we create when we act, and the change that happens to us when we don't.

Lorie Higgins, from Idaho, shared her experience with keeping ideas alive long enough to test them: I was talking to a friend about the idea [of pooling our money to buy and rehab downtown buildings], and she kept coming back with stuff like "I don't think we have enough people who can kick in enough money to buy even one building." I told her you discussed that's exactly how initiatives that could be effective get shot down before they are even explored and now she's in!

You have everything you need

When I was in North Central Illinois, a few people brought up issues holding them back. The city council is spending money on the wrong priorities. This foundation is giving money to the wrong things. There aren't any entrepreneurs in town, so we need to recruit from outside.

What if the answer to all of those is already at hand?

It doesn't matter what the council is doing. You don't need them. Go do your thing, starting by gathering a crowd. You don't need their permission or anything. Let them do their own thing.

It doesn't matter what the foundation is funding. You don't need money. It doesn't take any money to start conversations and Take Small Steps around the thing that matters most to you. If you think it takes money, your steps are too big. Take Smaller Steps.

You don't need outside entrepreneurs. You have your own people. They might be kids in school, families with lower incomes, or retired seniors, but you have potential entrepreneurs. Start with them.

Any time you think there is something you need, start by Gathering Your Crowd. You need a crowd so you can Build Connections. When you Build Connections, you build your network, and your network is where you find the resources you need.

It will never go back to the way it used to be

It will never go back to the way it was. We start from here and go forward.

You're the one who will start this change. You'll build the small steps and tiny experiments that will add up to change the shape of your town.

Think about applying this on different levels: yourself, your friends, your organization, your community. Then reaching out to more community leaders, regional groups, and others you can cooperate with in your state associations and memberships.

Your town has a future

Your town matters. It's worth the effort.

No place is quite the same mix of people and place, culture and heritage. You're unique. Despite all the naysayers, your small town has a future, and you're about to change it.

You've already started your Idea Friendly journey. You have a big idea. You know how to Gather Your Crowd. You're terrific at Building Connections, and you know how to Take Small Steps.

The method works because you work it. You don't need perfect conditions, unlimited resources, or everyone's permission. You need openness to new ideas and the willingness to start where you are with what you have.

Your community's future isn't controlled by a few organizations, leaders, or naysayers. It is created by you and all the people, each taking small actions every day. Your actions. Your willingness to stay open to new ideas. Your commitment to building community one small step at a time.

You're ready

You're joining a positive movement. You'll be part of shifting power in your town away from the hands of the few to the crowd. You've had enough of the old way, the Old Guard saying no to everything. You've had enough of suffocating under meaningless rules and pointless formalities.

You are the person who is best positioned to spark the movement in your town. Begin by using the three parts of the Idea Friendly Method:

Gather Your Crowd with your big idea, one that will bring people together to take action and improve your community.

Build Connections to turn that crowd into a powerful network and find resources.

Take Small Steps as you and your crowd accomplish the goal, each playing a small but meaningful role.

You can transform your community by taking small steps, starting now, without waiting for permission, support or perfect conditions.

Welcome to your Idea Friendly future. You've already begun.

Next steps: Get more Idea Friendly tools and resources online

Reach more people with videos, newsletters and more downloads

Use these resources to start your own Idea Friendly movement

You're not going ahead alone because you have these resources and tools. You're joining a positive movement that's bigger than your town. Like Abby in Miller, South Dakota, and Kathryn in Walla Walla, and thousands of others who are using this method to transform their communities. You're part of that movement. You'll find all these resources linked on the book's resource page at

saveyour.town/IFGuideResources

Free newsletters change your mindset and boost your group

Start with the email newsletters from Deb Brown and me. Even if you're desperately busy, these emails are your weekly dose of positivity. Just by reading them you're shaping your new Idea Friendly mindset.

Get your best friend, the one who'll help with anything you ask, to sign up for the newsletters, too. It gives you positive things to discuss together. You'll build up your Idea Friendly super powers.

If you're starting a positive action group, like in Chapter 7, these newsletters give you practical steps you can put into action right away. Each one gives you something positive to discuss at your next gathering.

One reader said: Goodday, I'm Stella Potgieter, a councillor in a small town, Koster, North West, South Africa. Thank you for all your ideas/tips that we receive through your newsletters. Koster is a small-ish town, with more than half of the community dependent on social grants, with no jobs. By watching you and getting ideas from you I hope to make a difference in our town as well as the rest of our municipality, in my term as councillor. Thank you, it's your positive outlook and ideas that make me go on.

Reach more people by showing this Idea Friendly Video in your town

You can share our 30 minute video on the Idea Friendly Method, called IF Our Town, to reach more people in your town. You can show it on your phone or tablet, or sit down together for a watch party.

From Mary-Elizabeth Harmon, PhD, Virginia: How do I love your Idea Friendly Method training? Let me count the ways: I love the clarity, substance & friendliness you packed into less than half an hour. I love the real world examples you shared.

TO ALL: If you're ready to take action on shaping a better future for your community, watch the Idea Friendly Method video.

Keep going with the First Ten Steps booklet

From simple ideas like Coffee and Calendars to more involved projects like pop-up festivals, this booklet walks you through it. You can share this with others to get them into action with you, without expecting them to go through this whole book first. You'll find it on the resource page, too.

Go more in-depth with videos on specific small town issues

You can learn more through our library of videos. Each one answers a specific real-world problem you may have in your town: improve housing, retain young people, find more volunteers, fill up downtown, find employees and more.

When you see how powerfully the videos can change people's behaviors, you'll want to reach more people. Invite a few friends to join you and watch together on your phone or laptop. Sharing videos gives you a positive reason to gather people that is not a formal meeting. Use the watch party tips from the resource download page, linked just above.

As your watch parties take off, you can turn them into a recurring event. Using the SaveYour.Town video library, you can target exactly the problems you most want to tackle. Members get access to dozens of videos on challenges like too many empty buildings, a downtown that is dead after hours or retaining young people.

Lorie Higgins from Idaho used our Idea Friendly videos as part of a Bootcamp for rural communities. She said, "I think you'll appreciate the impact story about Baker, Montana, that took the Idea Friendly Method to heart in their Bootcamp project. I continue to crow about the Idea Friendly Method whenever I have the chance!"

Lorie had details, too: Baker, Montana, population 1800, was part of that Idea Friendly Bootcamp and received $500 in seed funds. Knowing that rural communities that have arts organizations tend to be more innovative, they held an art walk as a way to Gather Their Crowd around the arts. They talked to everyone at the art walk to Build Connections and raised $800 with that event. Continuing with more Small Steps, they started a new arts organization and community theater group. The first theater production at Baker was a sellout and raised $21,000! They've used the Idea Friendly Method to build overwhelming community support for the arts.

Become certified in the Idea Friendly Method

Our Idea Friendly Toolkit includes more videos that go deeper into the method, the Idea Friendly Creed in a printable format, and an Action Guide workbook to help you implement what you've learned. Once you complete the toolkit, you earn a certificate that you can hang on your wall, share on LinkedIn, or wave around at the next city council meeting when someone says that won't work here. The certificate also visually connects you with other people across the country who are making their communities more Idea Friendly, just like you.

Get hands-on help in your community

When you're ready for hands-on help, you can bring Deb Brown or me for a visit. This generates more excitement and spurs action. It's an event, a focal point to Gather Your Crowd. Our view as outsiders means we're not biased by local history. You tap our personal knowledge of stories, examples and research that you can apply in your specific situation. We bring the concepts to the streets and help you with real-world application of the Idea Friendly method.

saveyour.town/workwithus

Add Idea Friendly presentations to your event

Bring me in for a presentation that is not some canned, old, boring thing. You've seen the topics I talk about, and I'll customize them to you. Add my down-to-earth advice to your local event, larger conference or virtual session. You get concrete take-aways that you can use today to shape the future of your town without getting beaten down by circumstances or others' negativity.

www.beckymccray.com

Download all the free resources for this book

This is your quick-list of what you'll find on the resource page at saveyour.town/IFGuideResources

1. Printable workbook called the Idea Friendly Action Guide to help you make notes and take action

2. Videos to share: The Idea Friendly video, the Rural Collaboration Webinar with SaveYour.Town and Dr. Dell Gines, a link to all our videos plus watch party tips

3. The Idea Friendly Creed from the front of this book, "We are a community of possibilities, not of problems..." Available in PDF and JPG for easy sharing.

4. "99% of the best things you can do for your community don't

require anyone's permission" full list of over 100 things to do

5. Old Way vs. Idea Friendly Way behavior chart

6. A "Success List" example from Carol Peterson

7. The First Ten Steps to an Idea Friendly Town

8. A reference list of books and research mentioned in this book

9. Discussion guide for groups (the book club questions that are in the next chapter)

Go download them now, before you leave this book. You'll find them all at the resource page:

saveyour.town/IFGuideResources

***

It will never go back to the way it used to be. We start from here and go forward.

You're joining a positive movement with all the people making their towns more Idea Friendly. We're all in this together. We're just in different towns.

You are the person who is best positioned to spark the movement in your town. Despite all the naysayers, your small town has a future, and you're about to change it.

Send that text.

Set that coffee date.

Post the Idea Friendly Creed and send me a picture.

Welcome to your Idea Friendly Town.

Discussion guide for groups

Hey, you could have a book club!

Adults learn by reflecting after doing something, so take action, then reflect.

Questions

- What was new to you?

- What resonated with you?

- What challenged you?

- How does the Idea Friendly Method compare to more formal programs you've been part of?

- What stories or examples excited you? Do you think they would work in your community?

- Were there any parts of the book that you found difficult to understand or follow?

- Did you take any action while reading the book, like texting a friend or changing how you do things?

- Is there an action you could take now?

- How would you describe this book to someone?

- What action will you take next?

- Who else do you think would benefit from this book? Are there organizations that would benefit?

- What unanswered questions do you have?

- Can you measure how this will impact your work or community?

Actions

Report back to me, especially actions you'll be taking, or things that could make the book more useful.

Group pricing

You can take advantage of special pricing for your group, and you can bundle this book with Deb's workbook *Save Your Small Town*. Just tell us what you'd like on the contact form at

SaveYour.Town/contact

Please leave a review

Even a one sentence review helps others

At our best, small town people support each other. If this book was helpful, your review helps the next community action-taker find it.

You can review it wherever you bought it:

saveyour.town/IFGuideBuy

Or on Goodreads:

saveyour.town/IFGGoodreads

Much appreciated!

Acknowledgements

Thanks beta readers, friends, and supporters

Special thanks to Deb Brown for all the stories I borrowed from her, and to Rob Hatch for the continual support throughout the process. You've both made my life richer for years and years.

A big rural SA-*LUTE* to the many beta and early readers who offered their support and some incredibly helpful suggestions:

Keri Holmes Rojas, Martha Brangenberg, Mick Samsel, Mysteri David, Rebecca Baer, Jamie Olmer, Jack Cunningham, Stephanie Olson, Sara M. Jondahl, Rick Brooks, Charlotte Knotek, Tonia Brookman, Karen West, Steve Sherlock, Kathryn Witherington, Catherine Holcomb, Becky Hansmeyer, Lavonne Sparling, Doug Brown, Natalie Muruato, JaNae K. Barnard, Jill Kuehny, John King, Sonya Nash, Jennifer Doyon, Melissa Fougere, Tim Parsons, Stephen Taylor, Jennifer Schenkenfelder, Melissa Halsell, Jackie Weiss, Delia Fey AICP, Dana Church, Christina Mortel, Mary Fant Donnan, David Burton, Dan, Jamie Beesley, Celia Simpson, Andrew Button, Maree Forbes, Danielle Steinhauser, Angela Brayham, Marci Goodwin, John C Shepard AICP, Ron Frantz, Debbie Saviano, Linda Foster, Carlton Shutt, Ruth Ann Skaggs, Joani Zoldowski, Margaret Dillard, Jackie Wolven, Mary Hamilton, Howard Pierpont, Kim Lozano, and Bob Hughes.

Thank you to you for reading this book, my newsletters, for sharing your ideas and stories with me and for caring about your own small community. You change the future.

About the author

Becky McCray has helped hundreds of rural communities discover they already have everything they need to thrive. A lifelong rural entrepreneur and cattle rancher, she's the co-founder of SaveYour.Town and creator of the influential Survey of Rural Challenges, used by businesses, organizations and educators since 2015.

Her hands-on experience as a retail business owner, city administrator, nonprofit executive and community volunteer—all in towns of 5,000 or fewer—gives her unique insight into what actually works in small places. She's collaborated with the American Independent Business Alliance,

Oklahoma State University's Rural Renewal Initiative, and Main Street America, and has presented at more than 300 events across the US, Canada, UK and Australia.

Becky makes her home in Hopeton, Oklahoma, a community of 30 people. Her goal is to deliver practical steps you can put into action right away to shape the future of your town.

Photo by Meg Hatch Photography, Maine.

Also by Becky McCray and SaveYour.Town

By Becky McCray and Barry Moltz

Small Town Rules

***

By Deb Brown

From Possibilities to Reality: Save Your Small Town

***

Coming soon from SaveYour.Town

Idea Friendly Solution Guides Series: Improving Rural Housing

***

Learn more at www.SaveYour.Town/books

www.ingramcontent.com/pod-product-compliance
Lightning Source LLC
Chambersburg PA
CBHW071603200326
41519CB00021BB/6856